## Also by Deborah Noyes

*A Hopeful Heart*
*Tooth and Claw*
*The Magician and the Spirits*
*Ten Days a Madwoman*

# Deborah Noyes

RANDOM HOUSE STUDIO ⌂ NEW YORK

Text copyright © 2022 by Deborah Noyes
Jacket art copyright © 2022 by Library of Congress Prints and Photographs Division,
LC-DIG-ppmsca-02180, LC-DIG-ppmsca-02505

All rights reserved. Published in the United States by Random House Studio,
an imprint of Random House Children's Books, a division of
Penguin Random House LLC, New York.

Random House Studio with colophon is a trademark of
Penguin Random House LLC.

Visit us on the Web! rhcbooks.com

Educators and librarians, for a variety of teaching tools,
visit us at RHTeachersLibrarians.com

Library of Congress Cataloging-in-Publication Data is available upon request.
ISBN 978-0-593-12203-7 (trade) | ISBN 978-0-593-12204-4 (lib. bdg.) |
ISBN 978-0-593-12205-1 (ebook)

The text of this book is set in 11.25-point Simoncini Garamond Std.
Book design by Andrea Lau

Printed in the United States of America
10 9 8 7 6 5 4 3 2 1
First Edition

*To CW—who showed me the sky*

# CONTENTS

*Benjamin Franklin's reception at the court of France, 1778*

# INTRODUCTION

In December 1776, a wily old American climbed off a boat onto the rocky coast of Brittany, France, with his two grandsons. The man was Benjamin Franklin, and he was malnourished, seasick, and exhausted, covered in boils and scabs. It had been a dark, turbulent winter voyage across the Atlantic, but his mission was urgent.

America was a British colony with a brand-new Declaration of Independence claiming the colony's right to govern itself. Armed conflict between British soldiers and bands of American colonists had begun in April 1775, and when the British crown sent its mighty army to crush rebellion in the colony, it fanned the flames of revolution.

England and France were old enemies, and Benjamin Franklin was making his way to the French capital to drum up support for what was evolving into America's fight for complete independence from Britain.

It wasn't Franklin's first trip to Europe, and he was already a celebrity among French aristocrats and intellectuals. They knew him not as an American statesman, patriot, and printer, but as the inventor who had tamed lightning—as a living symbol of the new, enlightened man of science.

Living by his wits in France and putting his social charms to work for the American cause, Franklin would coincidentally be on hand to witness startling scientific and technological advances over the eight years he would spend in the country. This would include a landmark human feat: "We think of nothing here at present but of flying," he wrote to a correspondent in London.

⟶  ⟵

Marie Madeleine-Sophie Armant, who would grow up to become Madame Sophie Blanchard, the world's first professional woman pilot, was just a few years old when the initial balloon flights took place in 1783. Her family lived 170 miles down the French coast from where woozy Benjamin Franklin had stepped off that boat in Brittany. A shy daughter of peasants, Sophie wouldn't make her mark on history for two more decades.

But to tell the story of a pioneering female balloonist, it turns out, you have to tell at least some of the early history of ballooning. That history begins in 1780s France, an impoverished nation barreling toward a bloody revolution. Like American patriots the decade before, oppressed French citizens were ready to demand liberty, equality, and justice for all.

The uprisings first in America and then in France were signs of the times, and few things were more revolutionary than balloons, which, as Victor Hugo, the author of Les Misérables, put it, freed humankind from the "tyranny of gravity."

When it hit in 1783, balloonomania (also known as balloon "fever" or balloon "influenza") took Europe by storm right alongside the violent political upheaval and social transformation that would set the stage for Sophie Blanchard's rise to fame.

For years to come, everyone would be talking about the new science of air travel ("aeronautics"), about the wondrous air transports and how they achieved flight ("aerostats" and "aerostation"), and about the brave men—and women—who flew in the face of gravity ("aeronauts").

There are very few original documents available that shed light on Sophie Blanchard's childhood and early years. I've reconstructed that part of her life based on what little we do know and in light of when and where she lived. For that reason, this book is very much a "life and times," with an emphasis on early flight, revolutionary politics, and the phenomenon of balloonomania.

Like early hot-air balloons, which were notoriously difficult to steer, this tale may drift a bit, both in the spirit of the subject and with the winds of historical context. But hold tight, and watch how a birdlike country girl became a high-flying celebrity, survived a revolution, and flew for an emperor and a king.

*Portrait of French balloonist Jean-Pierre Blanchard, 1785*

# CHAPTER 1

# A Mysterious Stranger

*March 1778*

Marie Madeleine-Sophie Armant, later known as Sophie Blanchard, was born March 25, 1778, in the remote hamlet of Trois-Canons, near La Rochelle, on the sunny west coast of France.

She would arrive in the world a few years before the first really big event of aeronautic history; but as the story goes, Sophie "met" her future husband and ballooning partner even before she was born.

➤ ◄

It was early springtime. Like all peasants bound to the land, Sophie's father would have been out tilling the fields, while her pregnant mother kept the family's humble inn. Peasants delivered an injured stranger to the inn that morning, an aeronaut on a makeshift stretcher. His balloon had crash-landed in a nearby meadow.

Peeled from a tangle of rope and deflated taffeta, the tiny spitfire of a pilot was battered and bruised but alive.

Over the coming days, the Armants offered Jean-Pierre Blanchard care and comfort, though the mysterious stranger had no money to repay their hospitality.

"Listen and mark my words," the airman told the couple on his way out, grinning at the mother-to-be who had so generously tended his injuries. "Fortune cannot always desert me. In sixteen years, if alive," he vowed, "I will return. If the child who will soon be born to you should be a boy, I will adopt him."

Exchanging a glance, his hosts chuckled politely.

"If a girl," Blanchard added, in that boasting tone of his, "I will marry her."

*Collector's card illustration of the first hot-air balloon ascent,*
*Annonay, France*

# CHAPTER 2

# The Race Is On

The First Recorded Hot-Air Balloon Flight
*Annonay, France; June 1783*

The First Recorded Hydrogen Balloon Flight
*Paris, France; August 1783*

A few years after that alleged crash landing in a field in Trois-Canons, Jean-Pierre Blanchard was in Paris, feverishly designing flying machines.

Like diplomat Benjamin Franklin, Blanchard was an inventor, and like Franklin and others in the capital at the time who were interested in scientific progress, he was keeping a close watch on the experiments of two brothers in the South of France.

Joseph-Michel and Jacques-Étienne Montgolfier were paper manufacturers with ties to King Louis XVI of France. Like many prosperous, educated European men of their day, they had the free time to be amateur or "gentleman" scientists.

The ingenious brothers had discovered a way of trapping heated air in a giant bag or balloon, and they were ready to test out their newfangled aerostat, or flying machine, in a public demonstration.

# Cloud in a Bag

Some say Joseph Montgolfier's vision for ballooning struck while he absently watched his wife's undergarments, pinned to a line near the fire, float up in the heat.

But the concept behind hot-air ballooning was already centuries old when Montgolfier connected the dots.

Two thousand years earlier, the Greek mathematician Archimedes had proposed, in his scientific treatise *On Floating Bodies,* that an object immersed in a fluid is lifted by a force equal to the weight it displaces.

By 1766, when two English chemists discovered hydrogen— they called it "inflammable air," a substance weighing just one-fourteenth as much as oxygen—scientists were beginning to see the implications for flight.

With Archimedes's principle in mind, Tiberius Cavallo, an Italian scientist living in England at the time, tried his hand at containing hydrogen in paper balloons. Since the substance was lighter than air, it stood to reason that the container would rise until its weight equaled that of the atmosphere around it. But the wily gas escaped through fibers in the paper, and Cavallo's balloons wilted.

*A creative portrait of Joseph Montgolfier, inventor of the hot-air balloon, anonymous artist, 1784*

Montgolfier picked up where his Italian colleague left off, filling paper—and later silk—globes with "inflammable air." But like Cavallo's before him, Montgolfier's creations floated only a few feet and then sank.

Seeking another lighter-than-air substance, one easier to contain than hydrogen, Montgolfier set out to mimic the way smoke and clouds rise in the atmosphere. His colleague's goal, wrote Cavallo, was to "enclose a cloud in a bag." The lifting cloud would then whisk the bag along with it.

But with no way to capture a cloud as a lifting agent, Montgolfier settled on smoke. He recruited his brother Étienne, and throughout early 1783, the enthusiastic brothers experimented with different combinations of cloth and paper for their envelope, inflating bigger and bigger bags.

By late spring of 1783, they had settled on a paper liner inside a strong linen balloon skin 110 feet around, with a volume of 22,000 cubic feet, and were ready to fill it with smoke—the smellier the better, Joseph believed. To supply the stink, he heaped everything from damp straw and wool to rancid meat and old shoes into the fire burner under the balloon.

What the Montgolfiers didn't yet know: it wasn't smoke that made the air in a balloon expand and rise; it was heat. The hot air inside is lighter than the cool air outside, causing the balloon to float up, as if in water.

On June 5, a lucky crowd collected in a field near Annonay's town square to bear witness. As the balloon's massive folds of fabric and paper filled with heat from a roaring fire, it must have seemed to them a strange sorcery.

The Montgolfiers' creation stirred, took form, and rose in a gelatinous mass with eight sweaty men holding fast to its open base. At Joseph's signal, the men set the straining balloon free, to a collective gasp from the audience.

To the amazement of the small crowd, the balloon sailed up some six thousand feet and floated for ten minutes before a waning current dropped it on terra firma a mile and a half away. Those present had just witnessed the first passengerless hot-air flight in history.

⇀ ↽

The moment news of the flight reached the French capital, the scientific community of Paris—including King Louis XVI and the Royal Academy of Sciences, as well as Ben Franklin and other visiting dignitaries from America—was abuzz. "The balloons engross all attention," Franklin wrote.

Jean-Pierre Blanchard surely also knew of the historic launch.

Born in 1753, he had fled rural Normandy as a young teenager, determined to escape the poverty he had grown up in. Small and scrappy, he was used to elbowing his way through the world and soon found work in Paris as a mechanic. In his free time, he invented things, though not all of his inventions succeeded. He was still a boy when he dreamed up

*Drawings of Jean-Pierre Blanchard's fanciful* vaisseau volant, *or "flying ship," 1784*

a rattrap built around a pistol, an ingenious hydraulic pump, and a type of velocipede, a forerunner of the bicycle.

Since the young inventor had lived in the capital, he had grown obsessed with flight and had begun designing winged flying machines, including what he called a *vaisseau volant* (a "flying ship" or "flying vessel") with foot pedals and hand levers that flapped four massive wings.

Not to be upstaged or outdone by the Montgolfiers in the south, Blanchard rushed out a bold, premature, and wildly exaggerated announcement in the *Journal de Paris:*

> *Within a very few days I shall be ready to demonstrate my own*
> *aerostatic machine, which will climb and dive on command,*
> *and fly in a straight line at a constant altitude. I shall be at the*
> *controls myself, and have sufficient confidence in my design to*
> *have no fear of repeating the fate of Icarus.*

But his ambitious airship never got off the ground.

For the time being, Jean-Pierre Blanchard was forced to step back and watch while the race to the skies went on . . . without him.

## The Fate of Icarus

In ancient Greek mythology, King Minos of Crete hired the master inventor, architect, and craftsman Daedalus to build an elaborate cage for the Minotaur, a half-bull, half-human monster. The labyrinth was so ingenious that no one could escape it, not even its maker— which Daedalus found out the hard way after helping a hero named Theseus slay the Minotaur and steal the king's daughter. King Minos, in a fury, shut Daedalus and his young son, Icarus, in the labyrinth.

Trapped in his own invention, longing for freedom and home, Daedalus despaired. Even if he devised a way out, he told his son, Crete was an island; the sea beyond was a prison, too.

"Minos rules all, Icarus," he said, "all but the heavens. We'll go that way."

Daedalus fixed feathers to a wooden frame with beeswax and built two intricate pairs of wings.

*Icarus and Daedalus*

As he suited Icarus up, the father warned his son not to fly too low and close to the sea. And to fly too high, too near the sun, would melt the wax. "Travel between the extremes," he urged. "Take the course I show you!"

But giddy Icarus soared away from his father, forgetting the warning. He flew higher and higher, flapping in vain while the sun melted the wax of his wings and his feathers fell. His bare arms slicing at the air, Icarus plunged to his doom while his anguished father cried his name.

Some claim that the villain in this story is pride, what the ancient Greeks called *hubris,* a cocky self-assurance offensive to the gods. Icarus overstepped. Others argue the boy was blissed out, so in love with the gift of flight that he lost his reason.

But the real villain of the story is gravity.

Encouraged by King Louis XVI and the Royal Academy of Sciences, a young physicist, Professor Jacques Charles, had set out almost at once to scientifically duplicate the Montgolfiers' experiment.

In a twist of fate that would make Charles the "father of the gas balloon," a newspaper report of the Montgolfiers' process mistakenly listed hydrogen instead of hot air as the balloon's lifting agent. The error led Charles and his partners, the Robert brothers, to develop a successful hydrogen prototype in the brothers' workshop in Paris.

There was just one small problem with the hydrogen balloon: hydrogen itself. As Joseph Montgolfier already knew, the gas escaped easily from light containers such as paper, silk, and animal bladders. Cooking it up in large batches was a slow, painstaking, costly, and potentially explosive process of injecting iron filings into casks of diluted sulfuric acid; as this acid-iron brew bubbled, hydrogen was forced through interconnected tin pipes.

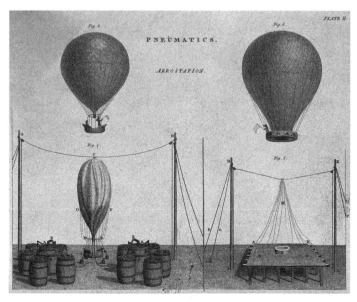

*Hydrogen (left) and hot-air (right) methods of filling a balloon*

While Charles and his team toiled behind the scenes, public excitement swelled. "Among our circle of friends," wrote one philosopher, "all one hears is talk of experiments, atmospheric air, inflammable gas, flying cars, journeys in the sky."

With king and country watching, the demonstration could not be put off much longer. After days of trial and error, Charles's weary crew finally got the pink-and-yellow balloon named the *Globe* fueled up and ready for takeoff.

On August 27, 1783, a restless crowd of more than fifty thousand flooded into Champ de Mars, the park that would eventually contain the Eiffel Tower.

A cannon sounded at five o'clock, and the men at the ropes released the balloon. To the spectators, who included Benjamin Franklin and young John Quincy Adams, who was in Paris at the time traveling with his diplomat father, the unpiloted ascent must have felt as if it were over before it began.

Adams recorded the balloon's progress in his diary: "It rose at once, for some time perpendicular, and then slanted. The weather, was unluckily very Cloudy, so that in less than 2. minutes it was out of sight: it went up very regularly and with a great swiftness." Franklin described the sight in a letter: "a little Rain had wet it, so that it shone, and made an agreeable appearance." The *Globe* shrank as it rose, seeming to Franklin "scarce bigger than an orange," and soon, "invisible, the clouds concealing it."

A companion turned to the American diplomat and asked earnestly, "What good is it?"

Franklin replied, "What good is a newborn baby?"

Forty-five minutes later, when a tear in the fabric released some of the balloon's hydrogen, the meandering *Globe*—with men on horseback in hot pursuit—touched down in rural Gonesse, fifteen miles northeast of Paris.

Adams concluded in his diary entry that the ongoing experiment in flight was an important one, "and if it succeeds it may become very useful to mankind."

But Franklin told his correspondent that the first unwitting—and terrified—specimens of humankind to see the twisting monstrosity, having never before seen or heard of a balloon, believed the deflating giant was alive, a beast, and they attacked it with stones and pitchforks.

"The creature, shaking and bounding, dodged the first blows," reported one Paris journal, but soon the balloon "received a mortal wound, and collapsed with a long sigh." A howl of victory sounded from the crowd, as one man inched forward and gave it a final stab with his dagger. The men lashed the giant corpse to a horse and dragged it roughly through the fields.

*Frightened villagers in Gonesse, France, attack Professor Charles's unpiloted hydrogen balloon, the* Globe, *when it lands on August 27, 1783.*

The incident prompted the French government to issue a proclamation—these "beasts" were for the betterment of humankind, a sign of progress—asking citizens who found grounded balloons in the future to stand down and notify the newspapers.

The sensational launches in Annonay and Paris were only the beginning of what would be, for many, an *Annus Mirabilis,* a year of wonders.

*The balloon launched by the Montgolfier brothers ascending from the Palace of Versailles, France, before the royal family, September 19, 1783, with a sheep, a duck, and a rooster aboard*

# CHAPTER 3

# Much Astonished

The First Recorded Hot-Air Flight with Animal Passengers
*Versailles, France; September 19, 1783*

Following up on Charles's successful hydrogen flight, King Louis XVI summoned the pioneering Montgolfier brothers to the royal palace at Versailles to demonstrate their hot-air machine.

Joseph politely declined, but Étienne Montgolfier had already arrived in Paris, in a spirit of cheerful competition, to follow Charles's progress. By September 14, just eighteen days after the ascent of the *Globe,* he had prepared his own spectacular balloon, seven stories high and oddly shaped, built over a platform that let hot smoke enter the balloon from a fire below.

In contrast to Charles's hydrogen balloon, which took four days to inflate, the vast Montgolfier, as hot-air balloons were now called, was full and straining after a mere ten minutes over a smoky fire.

But a rough wind ripped apart the clumsy giant, with the performance for the king and his court at Versailles just days away. Eager to win his monarch's favor and avert social disaster, the younger

Montgolfier brother raced to construct a new and simpler balloon: spherical, fifty-seven feet high, and forty-one feet in diameter.

While Paris awaited the latest spectacle, the city hummed with talk and opinions on the brave new science of "aerostatics"—and the tantalizing possibility of one day sending up a human pilot, an "aeronaut," to explore the mysteries of flight and weather.

Today's test flight would signal the way forward.

## The Dark Side of a Dream

If humans could fly, what next? The implications of "progress" were on everyone's lips, and for every bright-eyed enthusiast who supported advances in science and technology, there was a critic.

Some people worried that balloons would overturn the status quo. Smugglers would whisk contraband over the heads of customs officials. There would be warfare in the clouds. "They saw already armies slaughtering each other in the air and blood raining down on the earth," wrote one social observer. "Lovers and thieves might descend by chimney and carry away our treasures and our daughters."

Popular Gothic novelist Horace Walpole admitted, "All our views are directed to the air. Balloons occupy senators, philosophers, ladies, everybody." But balloons filled Walpole with foreboding. He feared they would be "converted into new engines of destruction,"

*Fictional balloon warships over a navy fleet*

18

like other scientific discoveries before them. "The wicked will of man always studies to apply the result of talents to enslaving, destroying or cheating his fellow creatures."

Even Benjamin Franklin, a balloon enthusiast, saw that airships could one day be put to military use. "Five thousand balloons capable of raising two men each," he calculated, "could carry a force of 10,000 troops rapidly into the field, crossing rivers, hills or even seas with speed and impunity."

But progress marched on, with or without society's anxious musings.

>-  -<

By ten o'clock on the morning of September 19, 1783, every avenue into Versailles was clogged with carriages or people jostling their way in on foot to witness a miracle.

"At last," one enthusiast wrote, "we have discovered the secret for which the centuries have sighed: man will now fly and so appropriate for himself all the power of the animal kingdom, master of the earth, the waters, and the air."

As if to demonstrate just how powerless the animal kingdom was in the face of human ingenuity, it would not be human aeronauts who reached the skies first; it would be a duck, a rooster, and a sheep named Montauciel ("Climb to the sky"), trapped together in a wicker cage.

The sheep earned the honors because his physiology approximated a human's. If poor Montauciel's head exploded at high altitudes, as many feared it might, humans were duly warned against air travel. The duck was a scientific control subject, unlucky but unlikely to be harmed since ducks, by nature, fly at high altitudes. The rooster, a bird that flies, though not high, was included as an additional control.

One way or another, analyzing the effects on the three passengers, Montgolfier and his science-minded supporters believed, would shed light on how flight might eventually impact humans.

Never had the royal palace at Versailles—or any place in France, for that matter—hosted such a grand spectacle for the public. Those on hand to cheer for Étienne Montgolfier and his balloon included King Louis XVI, Queen Marie-Antoinette, the royal family and courtiers, and some 130,000 spectators from all walks of life.

## Madame Déficit

Born an archduchess of Austria and the youngest daughter of Empress Maria-Theresa of Habsburg, Marie-Antoinette was a lively, frivolous, and homesick tomboy when she arrived at the Palace of Versailles at age fourteen to wed the future king of France. The marriage had been arranged by their allied families a dozen years earlier.

Escorted to her new country by an entourage of 57 carriages, 117 footmen, and 376 horses, the high-spirited Hapsburg princess won over the reigning king of France, Louis XV, at once. The king's grandson, however—Marie-Antoinette's shy fifteen-year-old bridegroom-to-be—was awkward and standoffish at first but would soon be deeply devoted to his bride.

Louis-Auguste, duc de Berry, and Marie-Antoinette were married on May 16, 1770, in the royal chapel at the lavish Palace of Versailles.

Three years later, on the morning of June 8, 1773, as King Louis XV lay ill, the dauphin and dauphine—or the future king and queen of France—made their first trip into Paris.

On the day of the event, known as the Joyous Entry, the vast city seemed to screech to a halt in the couple's honor. Livestock and beggars had been chased off streets strewn with flowers. The shops were all closed, and cheering multitudes—from aristocrats to apprentices, chimney sweeps to clergy—lined the streets hoping for a peek at their future rulers. They cheered and sang rousing ballads printed and distributed especially for the occasion, the merry clamor compet-

*Portrait of Marie-Antoinette by Jean-François Janinet, 1777*

ing with orchestral music and celebratory cannon fire. As the carriages of the royal entourage passed, a procession of soldiers and police fell in line and kept the pressing masses back with whips.

Louis XV died of smallpox less than a year later, elevating his weak-willed and retiring grandson to the most powerful throne in Europe. Louis and Marie were still teenagers—he nineteen, she eighteen—when they were put in charge of France at the most turbulent time in its history.

At first, their subjects embraced them. The young queen was bubbly and glamorous, though she was an outsider and disdainful of her responsibilities at court. As early as 1770, she complained in a letter, "I put on my rouge and wash my hands in front of the whole world."

Longing for escape and "terrified of being bored," Marie-Antoinette indulged in opera, theater, costume balls, gambling, and wild spending sprees. Where Louis was seen as lazy, immature, and unable to make up his mind—happier conducting scientific research, tinkering with locks, or winding his collection of clocks than directing affairs of state—Marie-Antoinette was lighthearted and impulsive, fond of games and sumptuous banquets, and quick to lavish political favor and financial gain on her private allies.

"My tastes are not the same as the King's, who is only interested in hunting and his metal-working," she confided to a friend in April 1775. Beyond extravagant, the queen's tastes included teetering bouffant hairdos, priceless jewelry, and a wardrobe of hundreds of glamorous gowns. The immature rulers soon found themselves in the eye of a social and political storm.

A string of wars and Louis's support of the American Revolution, a move to undermine his English enemy, had drained the French treasury, which was nearly bankrupt. Taxes were astronomical. Drought, failed harvests, and food shortages had sent the price of grain sky-high, and mobs of hungry people rioted regularly in the streets of Paris, chanting for bread.

Weary of an absolute monarchy where royalty had all the power at the expense of the people, and inspired by Enlightenment ideals of liberty, justice, and equality—as manifest in the newly independent United States—French citizens were beginning to discuss the possibility of self-government in more than a whisper.

Hidden away at Versailles, living a decadent and privileged life, the king and queen were clueless. Though Marie-Antoinette never uttered the infamous words "Let them eat cake," she was as mystified by the French public's hunger for democracy as she was by their physical hunger.

The young queen went right on gambling, hosting banquets, and purchasing diamond jewelry and silk finery. She invested a small fortune, some two million francs from the national kitty (about $6 million today), into renovating the château at Versailles known as the Petit Trianon—a three-story private getaway, or "pleasure house," reserved for Marie and her inner circle of friends. Those at court who were excluded grew envious and launched a campaign of petty backstabbing, scandal, and palace gossip that spilled out into the city to be satirized in radical antimonarchist pamphlets and racy cartoons.

Furious that she would waste the nation's money at a time of political and economic crisis, critics took to calling Marie-Antoinette "Madame Déficit."

More and more, the foreign queen became a scapegoat, hated and blamed for the nation's collapsing economy.

From the beginning, balloon ascents drew massive, restless crowds. To admit such a large crowd onto palace grounds was a major exception to protocol at Versailles. Rioting protesters had already broken through in 1774, the very first year of Louis XVI's reign, marching on the palace to demand fixed prices for flour and bread.

The royal debut of the hot-air balloon happened the same year that the Treaty of Paris was signed, signaling the end of the American War of Independence. Louis XVI had supported the American cause with both troops and money, an unpopular decision at a time when French citizens were (again) going hungry, and Louis and his queen now applauded the miraculous balloon ascent in their garden much as they might have cheered the faraway battles of American patriots, with no clue what lay ahead.

The royal corps of Swiss Guards stood by to defend Étienne Montgolfier and his creation if necessary. But beyond that, there was little effort to impose order on the thousands of spectators pressed into the courtyard to behold a miracle.

The festive event was staged not behind the royal palace but in the long park out front, where an octagonal platform had been built for *Aerostat Réveillon*. The balloon was a vast taffeta spheroid, sixty feet tall and sky-blue with golden fleur-de-lis.

At one o'clock in the afternoon, a drumroll sounded. The assembly fell silent, barring muffled objections from the barnyard aeronauts in their basket.

Slowly, majestically, the wobbling giant rose above a sea of uplifted faces.

When a gust of wind ripped the top of the balloon, many cried out, fearing for the safety of the animal passengers, but all three survived their eight-minute flight, which deposited them in a forest clearing beyond the palace.

Rumors spread among the crowd that the rooster's neck had been broken in the landing; others that its wing had been injured by a kick from the sheep. But a search party on horseback found the trio intact, the sheep nibbling on greenery, nonplussed, while his bird fellows paced nearby.

"It was judged that they had not suffered," one newspaper reported, "but they were, to say the least, much astonished."

*A pastoral country scene evoking Sophie's childhood home*

# CHAPTER 4

## Wide-Open Sky

*1783*

Sophie Armant was five years old when the first balloons took to the air. How she may have squealed with delight—or perhaps with worry; she was an anxious child—to see the barnyard trio float up in their little basket and disappear into the clouds.

But it's unlikely she witnessed the historic flight. Her hardworking family lived far to the southwest of Paris, in a tiny agricultural hamlet where men cultivated fields, raised livestock, or farmed oysters and mussels from the Bay of Yves. A trip to the capital would have taken several days in a rickety public stagecoach or "diligence," and longer by horse and cart.

Like many in France, the Armants were probably combating dire poverty in a year of volatile weather and failed crops.

# Year of Wonders

In the same season that humans defied gravity, a giant comet called a flying dragon streaked over Scotland, England, and France. Scientist Tiberius Cavallo recorded what he saw from the terrace of Windsor Castle that night: flashing lights "like the aurora borealis" emanating from "a roundish luminous body" half the diameter of the moon. For about thirty seconds, the bluish fireball of light moved with a rumbling noise "as it were of thunder at a great distance," and lit up "the whole face of the country. . . . Every object appeared very distinct."

For most of 1783, massive volcanic eruptions from the Laki fissure in Iceland wreaked havoc on the climate. The event lasted eight months and killed a fifth of all Icelanders, shooting sulfur into the atmosphere, staining the sky white with ash, and dusting Europe with acid rain. The hottest summer ever recorded was followed by a punishing winter. Crops failed and tens of thousands of people

*August 18, 1783, comet as seen from the balcony of Windsor Castle*

died from breathing the noxious smog that settled over many European countries, including France.

One contemporary described the "amazing and portentous" summer of 1783 as "full of horrible phaenomena . . . alarming meteors and tremendous thunder-storms that affrighted and distressed the different counties of this kingdom."

The eighteenth century was a time when science and reason were beginning to triumph over the superstition of earlier times, but in 1783, a great many people still saw unusual natural phenomena as ill omens, proof of God's disapproval. Comets, eclipses, and other solar events were linked to hunger, disease, and upheaval and they stoked panic.

Ballooning happened alongside turbulent economic and political events that would shape the French Revolution. It's no wonder people embraced the colorful diversion of ballooning, cheering its heaven-bound heroes at a time when hope was hard to come by.

Sophie was luckier than some peasant children in that she lived in a remote, sunny hamlet by the sea. It was a flat landscape of long sandy beaches, lazy rivers, and ancient salt marshes. In a normal year in Trois-Canons, she would enjoy mild winters and gentle breezes off the Bay of Biscay. Spring came early to the region, flooding nearby lagoons and making a home for greylag geese and whistling ducks and a place for storks to raise their young.

Terrified of horses, nervous Sophie no doubt avoided all large animals, but in spring and summer, when her chores were done—all children of working families, even very young ones, had chores—she could slip outdoors to hunt for newts among the buttercups or chase damsel-flies around bulrushes.

Perhaps the little girl collected orchids and irises that her mother kept in a milk bottle on a scuffed wooden table at the inn to cheer travelers. The Rivers Sèvre, Charente, Seudre, and Boutonne crisscrossed the region before they emptied into the Atlantic Ocean, creating a busy network of trade routes.

Perhaps, too, some of those travelers left behind wrinkled newspapers or chatted, while Sophie played on the floor with her dolls, about people and events in distant Paris: the indolent king and his selfish, pampered queen . . . hidden away from starving subjects in their fairy-tale palace at Versailles; miraculous balloons spiriting farm animals into the heavens.

Visitors didn't stay long in the Armants' quiet hamlet between the bustling seaports of La Rochelle and Rochefort, and this suited Sophie just fine. She was used to quiet and wide-open sky.

At low tide, the water in the bay retreated far out. There was room to run barefoot over the warm, wet sand, zigzagging with her arms wide, pretending to fly like the great flocks of birds that sometimes passed overhead, thousands and thousands at a time, on their migratory path. Did Sophie watch them and wonder? Did she imagine herself, even then, high above the clouds, away from hunger and fear?

Balloon used by Jean-François Pilâtre de Rozier and the Marquis d'Arlandes in ascent from Paris, November 21, 1783. The two men are just visible on the far edges of the wicker gallery.

## CHAPTER 5

# Perfect Bliss

First Piloted Hot-Air Flight
*Paris, France; November 21, 1783*

First Piloted Hydrogen Flight
*Paris, France; December 1, 1783*

The compulsory adventures of Montauciel the sheep and his feathered copilots now had France abuzz with the idea of putting *people* into balloons and sending them into the air. One good miracle deserved another.

Many adventurers, including Jean-Pierre Blanchard—who lacked the status and social connections necessary to get King Louis XVI's attention—now jostled for the privilege of being the first human to fly.

The monarch proposed sending up two condemned criminals ("much astonished" they would be!). If the men were lucky enough to survive their voyage, he argued, they would be pardoned.

One aspiring aeronaut complained, "The King might be sovereign master of my life, but he is not keeper of my honor. History should not be made by scoundrels but by men of distinction."

Jean-François Pilâtre de Rozier, an aristocratic twenty-nine-year-old doctor and professor of natural history, managed to win the king's favor with help from an army officer, the Marquis d'Arlandes, who was acquainted with one of Marie-Antoinette's ladies-in-waiting. The marquis used his influence in exchange for a seat in his friend's balloon.

After Rozier's first "captive" or tethered test run in Paris on October 15, 1783, to a cautious height of eighty-four feet, the trailblazer "assured his friends and the multitude, which had gazed on him with admiration, with wonder, and with fear," wrote a colleague, "that he had not experienced the least inconvenience, no giddiness, no incommoding motion, no shock whatsoever."

Rozier and d'Arlandes prepared to become the first human beings to take flight, quietly transporting the ornate blue-and-gold Montgolfier to the garden of the Bois de Boulogne palace, just outside the city.

*French balloonist Jean-François Pilâtre de Rozier, who took the first balloon flight in 1783*

November 21, 1783, the day of the flight, was gusty and overcast. Word of the ascent had spread quickly, and an excited crowd assembled while the aeronauts readied for liftoff. When a rogue wind rattled the massive sphere and tore it in several spots, the ground crew swiftly secured the balloon and made repairs as the audience grew more and more agitated.

From the beginning, balloons attracted restless crowds, often in the thousands or hundreds of thousands. Stirred up by advance publicity, and with no patience for the numerous techni-

*French balloonist Marquis François Laurent d'Arlandes, who took the first balloon flight in 1783*

cal variables involved in getting a vast balloon off the ground, audiences expected to be dazzled. False advertising, failed launches, and long delays often triggered riots, and many a balloonist beat a hasty retreat when the pressure was on. But today's crowd, the first to witness human flight, was breathless. Spellbound.

The wind died down at last, two hours later, with the seven-story Montgolfier poised to make history. Rozier and d'Arlandes stood on either side of the wide passenger balcony to evenly distribute their weight. A fire smoking in a wire-mesh basket above the balcony and just below the balloon's neck—with nearby pitchforks to heap bunched straw on the fire, water buckets and sponges at hand to tamp the fabric if it smoldered—would allow the men to control the balloon's ups and downs.

At 1:54, the ground crew released the ropes, and the balloon bobbed up. "I was surprised at the silence and the absence of movement among the spectators," d'Arlandes wrote afterward. The watchers seemed frozen in place, craning stiffly until the men far above flapped hats and handkerchiefs to break the spell and set the masses cheering and applauding wildly.

## Something Democratic About a Balloon

Rich and prominent citizens continued to secure the best seats in circular enclosures around balloon launch sites, but from the beginning,

*A massive crowd watches the launch of Professor Jacques Charles and Marie-Noël Robert's "aerostatic globe" from the Jardin des Tuileries, Paris, December 1, 1783.*

there was something democratic about a balloon. Try as balloonists might to reward their paying sponsors, outside the fragile bounds of "elite" enclosures, feverish crowds spilled into parks and courtyards and pressed into every available nook and cranny. People scaled walls and roofs to find better views. A balloon could not be kept a coveted secret, a pleasure for the fortunate few.

Balloons were for everyone, whether you were out plowing a field or sipping brandy on a palace balcony. The spectacle of a balloon brought people from all walks of life out in the open together to experience spontaneous wonder. They were young and old, peasants and aristocrats, priests and courtiers, male and female. "It is impossible to describe that moment," wrote one witness to a balloon launch, "the women in tears, the common people raising their hands to the sky in deep silence; the passengers leaning out of the gallery, waving and crying out in joy . . . the feeling of fright gives way to wonder."

The balloon, as historian Simon Schama put it, belonged to everyone in the crowd, not just the privileged. "On the ground it was still, to some extent, an aristocratic spectacle; in the air it became democratic."

The sedate giant sailed across the park and the River Seine at an elevation of about 280 feet, visible to all of Paris.

Because of the passenger setup—a wide circular wicker gallery with Rozier and d'Arlandes stationed on either side—the two men rarely saw each other while in flight, triggering a comedy of errors in the clouds.

Onlookers reported bits of repartee as the balloon drifted past overhead, with d'Arlandes chanting some variation of "We must go down!"

When the balloon seemed to be sinking at one point, Rozier barked at his companion to quit admiring the view and stoke the fire. "Let's work! If you keep gaping at the Seine we'll be swimming in it soon."

Less unflappable than his captain, d'Arlandes fretted away the flight. Would the balloon catch fire? Would the canopy jar loose? Would all the balloon cords snap and send the gallery hurtling? "We must land now!" he cried repeatedly. When the vessel shook at one point in a fierce gust, d'Arlandes howled, "What are you *doing*! Stop dancing!"

Fearless Rozier gamely removed his green topcoat, rolled up his sleeves, and set to work feeding the flames. "Look, d'Arlandes," he teased. "*Here we are above Paris.* There's no possible danger for you. *Are you taking this all in?*"

The men traveled roughly five miles in twenty-five minutes, until fire burned holes "of considerable size" in the balloon fabric. While they were sponging out the flames, two of the cords connecting the gallery to the balloon snapped, and the balloon dropped at a slant, nearly brushing the rooftops of Paris as the men hurled straw on the fire, lifting themselves to safety in the nick of time.

When the balloon landed near two millhouses, Rozier leaped out first and wistfully watched it collapse. "We had enough fuel to fly for an hour," he lamented as a crowd quickly formed.

There was still plenty to celebrate, so Rozier handed around the basket of provisions. But his welcoming committee seized the hero's green topcoat instead and began tearing it to bits for souvenirs.

Later, Rozier reported "no shock whatsoever" during the flight. He became known as "the intrepid Pilâtre, who never loses his head." Though the hot-air Montgolfier was a clumsy giant, a devil to control, the flight had been a grand success.

But an even bigger balloon sensation was already forming in the wings.

➤ ◄

Since his previous balloon, the *Globe,* had met its inglorious end under the knife blades and pitchforks of frightened peasants, Professor Jacques Charles and his partners were busy toiling away in the Robert brothers' Paris workshop on a follow-up hydrogen design to rival the giant Montgolfier.

Charles's new balloon had a long wicker basket that hung safely from ropes under its canopy, an envelope or "skin" made of silk, coated on the outside with tough rubber and draped in netting, and a gas valve at the top for letting out air when it was time to land. A ballast system of weighted sandbags allowed for better control of the balloon's ups and downs. The trio had worked out an efficient design that would serve balloonists for centuries to come.

On December 1, 1783, ten days after Rozier's pioneering hot-air trip, Charles was ready to outshine his rival in a spanking-new red-and-white-striped hydrogen balloon, twenty-six feet in diameter.

## Eighteenth-Century Crowdfunding

Hundreds of Parisians helped finance Charles's balloon through a "subscription." In exchange for their donations, supporters gained admission into a special enclosure around the balloon. What one early balloonist called "a tax on the curiosity of the public" earned them the best seats in the house.

*Admission ticket to a Vincent Lunardi balloon ascent, 1784*

Though some balloonists enjoyed government support, the majority needed patrons to help them aloft. Balloonists also made money to fund flights by selling a coveted passenger seat.

The launch attracted some 400,000 spectators from all around the city and the surrounding countryside. They flooded into the Jardin des Tuileries and spilled out of the public garden and into the streets. They lined rooftops and clogged the quays of the River Seine. It was one of the biggest crowds Paris had ever hosted.

Hundreds of elite subscribers had paid an admission fee to stand inside the balloon enclosure. Balloon enthusiast Benjamin Franklin was a subscriber, but he wasn't feeling well that day so opted instead to watch the launch from his carriage through a pocket telescope.

Étienne Montgolfier was present, and Professor Charles honored the now-famous inventor by inviting him to release the five-foot pilot balloon that would test the day's wind and weather conditions. "It is for you, *monsieur*," Charles said graciously, "to show us the way to the skies."

While the crowd watched the bright green test globe sail off to the northeast, Charles and his copilot, Marie-Noël Robert, hopped into a basket decked out with furs, blankets, and champagne. When the cannon boomed, they dumped out nineteen pounds of sand, and the great globe rose majestically to two hundred feet, leaving the audience spellbound.

"Nothing," Charles wrote later, "will ever equal that moment of joyous excitement which filled my whole being when I felt myself flying away from the earth. It was not mere pleasure; it was perfect bliss."

The men waved white pennants to the multitudes below, and Paris seemed to hold its collective breath. Nearly half the city's population had spilled into the narrow streets surrounding the public garden, and once the gaping masses saw that the men were safe, their applause was deafening.

High in the clouds, Charles and Robert studied barometers, hurled out articles of clothing and blankets to lighten the load as needed, and vented hydrogen to keep a constant altitude.

When distant cannon fire sounded to signal that they were out of sight of Paris, "we gave ourselves up," Charles wrote, "to the views which the immense stretch of country beneath us presented," eventually alighting in a field twenty-seven miles from the Tuileries.

After Robert climbed out, relieving the balloon of weight, Charles was inspired to soar up again, seizing renown as the world's first solo aeronaut. "I passed in 10 minutes from the temperature of spring to that of winter," he recorded. "I examined all my sensations calmly. I could hear myself live, so to speak."

Charles took barometer readings to judge altitude, and topped out at nearly ten thousand feet. "I was the only creature on the horizon in sunshine," he wrote, for he had climbed high enough to see the sun again, though it had set for those on the ground, leaving "all the rest in shade."

While he enjoyed his second sunset of that momentous day, the abrupt change in air pressure brought on a crippling pain in his right ear and jaw, at last prompting Charles to release gas from

*French balloonist Professor Jacques Charles, the first to fly solo in a hydrogen balloon, several years before his historic 1783 ascent*

the balloon and drop ballast to return to earth, coasting to a moonlit landing in a field.

Professor Charles later published a popular account of his flight, which "was not a mere delight," he reported, "but a kind of physical rapture." Though he kept up his studies of the science of flight, he would never fly again.

*Jean-Pierre Blanchard and his balloon, around 1783*

# CHAPTER 6

# The Naked Aeronaut

Debut Flight of Jean-Pierre Blanchard
*Paris, France; March 2, 1784*

While Sophie, who was still a child, would not have witnessed Charles's balloon lift, or Rozier's, it's very likely that Jean-Pierre Blanchard, the man she would one day marry, did.

Not long after the air race began, Blanchard had abandoned his doomed *vaisseau volant,* or flying ship, and tossed his hat into the ballooning ring.

Even as Charles became the toast of France, Blanchard was hard at work on his own hydrogen balloon design.

At thirty-one years old, the ambitious inventor announced his first flight, which would launch from Champ de Mars in Paris on March 2, 1784.

Terrible with money, and lacking the social connections of rival aerial adventurers, Blanchard made up for the dearth of funds and friends in high places with bluster and advertising. He was still feverishly experimenting with methods of navigation, from aerial oars and rudders to a simple hand-cranked propeller with eight-foot blades, and he believed his latest innovation, a set of flapping silk wings stretched over a wicker frame, would steer his vessel through the air as you might steer a ship through water. With no evidence to back up the boast, Blanchard vowed in advance publicity to both pilot his craft and navigate the upper air.

Blanchard had booked an unusual companion for his debut flight, a renegade monk named Pesch whose order had forbidden him to travel in the "invention of the Devil." Brother Pesch had braved imprisonment—and no doubt paid a hefty sponsorship fee—for the chance to fly, but he never made it into the balloon that March day, much less off the ground.

In fact, Blanchard's momentous first flight almost didn't happen at all. Famously arrogant and disagreeable, the aeronaut got into a scuffle with a gentleman who wanted a seat in his balloon. The spurned passenger lashed out, slashing at the craft's oars and rigging with his sword and wounding Blanchard's hand before police apprehended him.

Eluding both Pesch and an impatient crowd, Blanchard lifted off without any passenger at all.

It would become his modus operandi: ditching sponsors whenever he could to claim the spotlight—and the glory—for himself. But there would be little glory this time. By brashly predicting the course of his flight, he had set himself up for failure.

His proposal to "row" northeast to La Villette, a Paris park, went awry when a teasing wind whisked his balloon off course and across the River Seine.

Paris had a good laugh at his expense that day.

➤ ◄

Blanchard followed up his first flight with two launches in his native Normandy that spring and summer.

Balloon pilots were customarily greeted by cheering multitudes—crowds eager to assist and celebrate them when they landed—but Blanchard's third flight brought him down in a field among baffled peasants.

## Men or Gods?

It wasn't just balloons themselves that were *en vogue*. Aeronauts, those who piloted the flying globes, became romantic heroes. People met them after a launch with earnest flattery, asking, "Are you men or gods?" Bystanders flocked to a balloon wherever it landed (and as Jean-Pierre Blanchard learned the hard way, it was tough to know precisely where a balloon would land . . . it was largely up to the wind) to cheer and assist them.

"Covered in sweat and smoke [the aeronauts were] constantly stopped on their progress," reported another observer, "by those who wanted to see them up close and embrace them."

Merchants in Paris or at

*People rush to assist Jacques Charles at his landing, 1783.*

market fairs around the country sold mini portraits of the airmen and printed sheets of ballads narrating their exploits. Strangers feared for them in the air and toasted them on the ground, offering them seats at their tables and hearths, welcoming them like family. Ballooning inspired a feeling of fellowship that crossed class boundaries.

Certain he was from outer space, the peasants poked and prodded him, and were only satisfied that he was human when he took off every stitch of his clothing.

At least the audience at Blanchard's landing didn't tear his clothes to bits, like Rozier's green topcoat. But it was far from the hero's welcome that his lofty predecessors had enjoyed. Short on charm but tireless and inventive, the ornery pilot would need to step up his game to compete.

*A fashionable lady takes in the latest balloon spectacle.*

# CHAPTER 7

# Castles and Arias in the Air

## The First Woman Takes Flight
### *Lyon, France; June 4, 1784*

Almost immediately after Charles's historic and highly publicized adventure in the clouds, ballooning became a national obsession, a "fever" of epic proportions. People were giddy with "balloonomania," and throughout the eventful summer and fall of 1783, the latest flight was all the rage, and the mania fanned out from France to other countries.

In Paris, the colorful flying globes inspired trends in clothing, hair, jewelry, and home decor. Shops overflowed with fashionable "balloon bonnets" and silk fans illustrated with airships. Balloons appeared on birdcages and clocks, tobacco cases and candy boxes, wallpaper and furniture. Craftsmen

*An ornate, balloon-inspired fan
from around 1783*

shaped elegant crystal chandeliers like balloons and engraved the globes on sword handles and medallions. Balloons became a popular entertainment theme in theaters, dance halls, and fairgrounds.

The romance of ballooning captured the imagination of famous fiction writers like Jules Verne and Victor Hugo. Journalists satirized the fad, along with its devotees and fashionistas, in editorials and madcap cartoons of floating cities and balloon-butted ball gowns.

To feed the frenzy, Parisian publishers printed books and pamphlets with step-by-step advice for constructing working mini balloon replicas from animal bladders and fish glue. Fashionable hosts released tiny fruit-shaped balloons after dinner to entertain their guests, and Benjamin Franklin sent minis home to America and to scientific friends in England.

## Do-It-Yourself Fire Balloons

Though no one was exactly an expert in the infant field of aeronautics, some were more amateurish than others. Burning trash, Montgolfier style, to create hot smoke earned the hot-air balloon the nickname "fire balloon." Accidents happened with alarming frequency. In October 1784, a flaming balloon fell "on a building at the fair of St. Laurent," one newspaper reported, "where wild beasts were kept for show, such as lions, tigers, &c." Luckily the blaze was contained before tragedy struck.

Handling hydrogen was no safer than heating air. Sixteen-year-old John Quincy Adams wrote home that the "flying globes are still very much in vogue. They have advertised a small one of eight inches in diameter at 6 livres apiece without air [hydrogen] and 8 livres with it. . . . Several accidents have happened to persons

*A balloon catches fire, 1784.*

who have attempted to make inflammable air, which is a danger-ous operation, so that the government has prohibited them."

→ ←

How might Sophie and her family, hungry peasants living in rural isolation, have known about balloons or felt their cultural influence? The Armants ran a country inn, of course, so balloons may have come up in conversation with travelers returning from or heading north to La Rochelle or Paris. Their customers might have left behind news-papers or pamphlets—though much of agricultural France, particularly in the south and particularly women, was still illiterate—but the printed illustrations might have been enough to stop the Armants in their tracks, even in the course of a busy workday. Balloons smacked of the fantastic. They were visually striking and deliciously strange.

Another way the family might have learned of balloonomania was at one of the markets held in larger towns or meadow fairgrounds all over France and Europe.

*A man pasting advertisements, including one for a balloon launch, on the side of a building, 1870*

While her father bartered for necessary market goods, Sophie and her mother might have wandered about to watch an organ-grinder's monkey, taken in a Punch and Judy puppet show, or inspected bolts of silk laid out on boards in splendid colors. They might have browsed stalls heaped with printed linens and ostrich-plume hats, admired shelves of bottled perfumes and medical potions, or chatted with saucy parrots in bamboo cages. They might also have noticed advertisements plastered to the walls of buildings, or happened across a table of books and prints.

Etchings and single-sheet prints were a popular way to advertise or commemorate events at the time. To illustrate what a balloon looked like for the public—and narrate the heroics of aeronauts—artists, engravers, and printers rolled out images of balloons by the thousands. Some were exact and mechanical. Others were flights of fancy.

*Fanciful design for an aerostat*

Did Sophie pore over these pictures with the same wonder and curiosity she might have felt looking up at the great old castle of the Courbon family on the cliffs above the River Bruant near her home? Did she learn early to dream of castles and balloons in the air?

## Hunger and Rags

Ladies with balloon-shaped ball gowns would have seemed dangerously frivolous (as did the extravagant queen, Marie-Antoinette, with her sky-high hair and jeweled gowns) to the average peasant in 1783 France. A revolution was brewing that would soon tip the social balance, but many of the nation's hungry citizens owned only one wretched set of homemade clothes for all seasons, coarse cloth or wool colored black with dye from the bark of the oak tree (black to double as a mourning outfit). A man owned a single pair of shoes—a common wedding gift—that had to last a lifetime, while most women and children went barefoot. "A French peasant is badly dressed," wrote one observer, "and the rags which cover his nudity are poor protection against the harshness of the seasons."

*Peasants solemnly consider their yield.*

As a child, Sophie must have found fleeting chances to daydream, to imagine herself in glittering faraway Paris among royal courtiers in silk and ostrich feathers—or drifting above the snaking River Seine and the cathedrals, palaces, and gardens of the city in a dainty basket. But if balloons did fuel Sophie's early dreams, there was good news to come.

In the early summer of 1784, not two years after Joseph Montgolfier invented the hot-air balloon and eight months after the first piloted air flight, nineteen-year-old Élisabeth Thible of France became the first woman to copilot an untethered balloon.

At a time when women rarely got to engage in work or play—especially dangerous play—outside the domestic sphere, the idea of a woman taking wing for thrills was unheard of; but on June 4, 1784, Élisabeth Thible convinced a painter friend to take her up on a hot-air flight. The amateur aeronaut, one Monsieur Fleurant, was scheduled to go up from Lyon in *La Gustave*—a balloon named for King Gustav III of Sweden, who was visiting France at the time—with his friend Count Jean-Baptiste de Laurencin. When the friend suffered nerves, Thible won his seat.

Other women had floated up in tethered balloons, but when Thible stepped aboard the balloon for a free flight dressed as the goddess Minerva, the stunned crowd went wild. She and Fleurant sailed up with style, singing operatic arias in the clouds, and despite a bumpy landing that twisted her ankle, their flight was a sensation.

Thible had shown great daring in the air, Fleurant reported, feeding the firebox and otherwise carrying her weight as copilot. Count de Laurencin applauded his replacement in a letter to Joseph Montgolfier himself. "A thousand persons of her sex, have shown us that courage is not solely a male attribute; but I assert that no woman has furnished better proof." Thible paved the way for future female aeronauts at a time when women had very few opportunities to compete on equal terms with men.

To a young girl like Sophie, grounded in a tiny village by the sea, eavesdropping on travelers as she wiped down tables at the family inn, the skies above France must have seemed limitless indeed.

*A lively depiction of Jean-Pierre Blanchard and Dr. Jeffries arriving in Calais, France, after crossing the English Channel in a hot-air balloon, 1785*

# CHAPTER 8

# A Perilous Crossing

Blanchard and Jeffries Fly over the Channel
*Dover, England; January 7, 1785*

Tired of being eclipsed by better-financed celebrity aeronauts like Rozier and Charles, and feeling ridiculed and sidelined after his Paris debut, Jean-Pierre Blanchard took his one-man balloon show on the road. By 1785, he had traveled all over Europe giving demonstrations and developing a name for himself as one of the world's best-known "professional" balloonists.

Renowned as the first to fly a balloon in Germany, Poland, the Netherlands, and Austria—and increasingly skilled in self-promotion, advertising, and publicity—Blanchard now had little trouble attracting sponsors. His reputation preceded him, and the growing popularity of ballooning in England—thanks to a glamorous young Italian named Vincenzo "Vincent" Lunardi who was living and flying in London at the time—inspired Blanchard to break new ground there.

The next great challenge, he believed, was to fly a balloon across the English Channel (*La Manche* to the French). All he needed was an eager sponsor.

## Ballooning in Britain

The first balloon to fly over England was sent up by an Italian. On November 4, 1783, with little to-do, Count Francesco Zambeccari launched a small, unpiloted hydrogen balloon from a London rooftop. People rushed out to marvel as it sailed over the city, but it was a quiet affair as balloon ascents went, and his later efforts ultimately left him disgraced when a highly publicized flight fell through and his audience rioted.

Scottish apothecary and encyclopedia editor James Tytler was the first to pilot a balloon over Britain, flying from Abbeyhill to a town outside Edinburgh on August 27, 1784.

By September, thirty-year-old Italian Vincent Lunardi prepared to launch from English soil. He funded his red-and-white-striped balloon by displaying it at the Lyceum Theatre in the Strand, London, where it hung from the ceiling for several weeks.

Lunardi charged an entrance fee for a peek at the balloon and sold gallery seats for the launch itself. Some twenty thousand visitors flowed through to see the balloon, and Lunardi, a born showman, was soon the darling of London. Handsome and flirtatious, he eagerly as-

*Italian balloonist Vincent Lunardi, the first aerial traveler in England, with his pets*

sumed the role of romantic aeronaut for his adopted countrymen and -women. Lunardi commissioned a formal portrait with his pet dog and cat, and vowed publicly to take them up in the air with him.

Lunardi wrote that "about one hundred and fifty thousand spectators" showed up for his ascent, "composed of all ranks and descriptions of people." The crowd filling the artillery field at London's Moorfields threatened to riot when takeoff was delayed by just a couple of hours, but when the balloon finally ascended, the circle of elite subscribers in the gallery rose to their feet to watch, utterly silent, gravely doffing their hats.

Lunardi glided northwest with pets in tow, feasting on chicken legs and champagne and periodically "rowing" his balloon with aerial oars no doubt modeled on Blanchard's prototype. After a while, as he told it later, his little cat began to shiver, and the gallant aeronaut was obliged to paddle to earth and pass his precious cargo to a young lady in a field. Then he dropped ballast and sailed up again.

On the spot where he finally did land, he raised a monument reading:

> Let posterity know, and knowing be astonished, that on the 15th day of September 1784 Vincent Lunardi of Lucca in Tuscany, the first aerial traveller in Britain, mounting from the artillery ground in London and traversing the regions of the air for two hours and fifteen minutes, in this spot revisited the earth.

Lunardi was scarcely out of his balloon when London's presses began to roll. He sold exclusive rights to his account of the flight, became the subject of popular ballads, and inspired fashion accessories (including a ladies' garter named in his honor). He dined with aristocrats, met the king, and wrote home to Italy: "I am the idol of the whole nation."

Following Lunardi's lead, balloons—piloted and unpiloted, with passengers and without—went up all over the United Kingdom—in London, Oxford, Cambridge, Bristol, Edinburgh, and other cities.

Blanchard settled in England, built a medium-sized hydrogen balloon, and began to hunt up sponsors.

Dr. John Jeffries was American, a Boston-born doctor who had remained loyal to the British crown, fleeing to London during the American Revolution. Jeffries agreed to finance the Frenchman's Channel crossing—in exchange for a seat in his basket.

The doctor would secure the honor of being the first American to go up in a piloted balloon, but Blanchard would test his determination. The aeronaut needed Jeffries to fund the expedition but had no desire to share the glory. Famous for his temper and greed for the spotlight, Blanchard had already tricked previous benefactors out of their seat in his balloon and earned a reputation for hurling scientific instruments overboard as ballast.

*Portrait of American balloonist Dr. John Jeffries, 1786*

The official launch would be from the grounds of Dover Castle on the English coast, and as

Blanchard made preparations, he tried to shut Jeffries out of his base camp, barricading himself inside the castle.

His outraged sponsor paid a party of sailors to storm Blanchard's fortress and clear the way for Jeffries and his equipment. He also enlisted the castle governor to broker an uneasy agreement between the two balloonists.

Once the balloon was inflated, on January 7, 1785, pilot and passenger loaded up the gondola with Blanchard's useless hand propeller and oars (steering, as the aeronaut had learned on his first voyage, was next to impossible; but he kept trying, and the oars looked impressive), anchor, sandbags for ballast, cork jackets as life preservers, promotional leaflets, Jeffries's scientific equipment, food, and brandy.

But Blanchard schemed up until the bitter end to trick Jeffries out of his seat.

When it came time to lift off, they exceeded weight limits. With both men aboard, the balloon was too heavy to rise. They would have to settle it like gentlemen, Blanchard reminded his passenger, as they had agreed in advance. He graciously offered to forge on alone for the good of the expedition.

Immediately suspicious, Jeffries foiled the plot by demanding to inspect the pilot's clothing. Clever Blanchard had managed to attach a series of heavy lead weights to a leather belt under his waistcoat.

At 1 p.m., the hydrogen balloon set sail over the white cliffs of Dover with both men aboard.

## Science or Spectacle?

From the beginning, the French had few doubts about the benefits of ballooning. The country's aeronauts often enjoyed government funding, and many of the first flights were considered scientific "experiments." Balloonists would one day demystify the weather, observe the stars, explore the planet, carry out military reconnaissance, and transport heavy cargo.

But balloonomania spread more slowly across the Channel, despite Benjamin Franklin's challenge to Sir Joseph Banks, the president of Britain's Royal Society, which was the center of scientific study in the United Kingdom.

In the matter of "aerostation," Franklin wrote to Banks,

*Portrait of Joseph Banks, circa 1810*

"your philosophy seems too bashful." Why was England's formal scientific community holding back?

Banks saw the draw of ballooning but felt it was too unpredictable to serve science. Balloonists might use scientific instruments to clock height and air pressure, or "experiment" to see if their sense perceptions and mental faculties changed at higher altitudes, but navigation remained elusive. They were bound by the mysteries of the upper air currents to deliver them . . . somewhere . . . and there was no room for unreliability in science. As another Royal Society member (and author of the first English history of ballooning), Tiberius Cavallo, put it, too often aerial voyages made "for the improvement of science" were "performed by persons absolutely incapable of accomplishing this purpose." Most balloonists went up for "the sake of the prospect," for the money, or to "add their names to the list of aerial adventurers."

"Dr. Charles' experiment seems decisive," Banks told Franklin, referring to Professor Charles's much-discussed hydrogen flight sponsored by the French crown; but when Britain's King George III asked Banks if research into "air globes" should be officially sanctioned, the scientist replied that "no good whatever" could result from such experiments. The French had a habit of mistaking novelty for real science, Banks hinted.

The English public was divided. Some saw ballooning as a passing fad, including London's *Morning Herald,* which urged England to "laugh this new French folly out of existence as soon as possible." But the cynics couldn't hold back the tide of popular opinion, and balloonomania had already crossed the Channel.

Sophie Armant was only eight when her future husband sailed over the Channel. While she swept the dirt floor of her family's kitchen or lugged water from the well, Blanchard and an enchanted American scientist voyaged two hours over sea and forty-seven minutes over land with flags flying, one English and one French, to thunderous applause on either shore.

Heavy with equipment and supplies, the balloon began to lose altitude at one point and nearly dropped into the Channel. "My noble little captain gave order, and set the example," Jeffries wrote later.

Blanchard furiously dumped ballast and, when all the sand was gone, started chucking flight equipment. Down went the propeller, the oars, the anchor, "after which my little hero stripped and threw away his coat. On this I was compelled to follow his example. He next cast away his trousers. We put on our cork jackets and were, God knows how, as merry as grigs to think how we should splatter in the water."

In the nick of time, the lightened balloon began to rise and level out, and at 3 p.m., "benumbed with cold," the men spotted the French shoreline.

Careening again over the Felmores forest in Calais, France, twelve miles inland, both men peed over the side to further relieve the balloon of weight. "Almost as naked as the trees," without "an inch of cord or rope left, no anchor or anything to help us," Jeffries wrote, they touched down in a clearing around 3:30 p.m., shivering and dizzy with triumph.

Spectators crowded around with articles of clothing, relaying the hastily clad aeronauts by carriage to Calais for a hero's welcome, followed by celebrations in the capital. Jeffries received no reward beyond the admiration of "hundreds of the first ladies and gentlemen of Paris." But Blanchard must have appreciated the poetic justice when his monarch, King Louis XVI, proclaimed him a patriot and granted him a royal pension.

*An illustration of the perilous landing of Major Money, an aeronaut who crashed into the waves off the coast of Yarmouth, England, but was rescued seven hours later*

# CHAPTER 9

# However Dangerous or Difficult

The First Balloon Fatalities;
Women Flock to the Skies
*1785*

While Blanchard and Jeffries were being toasted in Paris, the daredevil doctor Jean-François Pilâtre de Rozier was feeling the squeeze. He politely congratulated his colleagues but had been laboring for weeks on a government-funded voyage across the Channel in the opposite direction, crossing from Boulogne, France, to England, and his royal sponsor was impatient.

Bad weather and rough winds delayed Rozier's launch further, but after several false starts, five months after the Blanchard-Jeffries crossing, he and his balloon's builder, Pierre Romain, would attempt the perilous crossing from France to England in a mixed-hot-air-and-hydrogen balloon, a model now known as a Rozier.

As one of the first men to fly, Rozier was no stranger to risk. He had also been the first to prove that hydrogen was flammable by boldly inhaling it, then exhaling into an open flame, scorching his eyebrows in the bargain.

*French professor and balloonist Jean-François Pilâtre de Rozier blows hydrogen gas into a flame.*

As a scientist, he understood the grave risk of combining hydrogen and fire in the same craft. Though the elements were employed separately in his balloon design, their proximity alone was treacherous.

He and Romain kept up a confident front. Rozier had vowed on his honor to make the flight and would not refuse his king. But he confided to friends that he was "certain of meeting with death" on this ill-advised voyage.

About twenty minutes into the June 15, 1785, flight, reports began circulating on the ground that a valve rope was slapping against the upper part of the balloon.

One slap had generated static electricity and ignited the hydrogen.

Flames spurted from the balloon's crown as massive crowds along the coast looked on—including Rozier's horrified young fiancée, Susan Dyer—and the balloon burst in "a violet flame."

One viewer later described the disaster to a correspondent: "When they were at an amazing height, the balloon took fire, burnt the cords by which the car was suspended, and the above gentlemen were dashed to pieces in a manner too shocking to mention."

Rozier and Romain fell fifteen hundred feet onto rocks outside the port, their bodies violently shattered.

# A Little Chilled

Many deemed it a miracle that the deaths of Pilâtre de Rozier and Romain were the first.

Balloons had the power to destroy lives on the ground, too.

In May of the same year, the world's first full-scale aviation disaster occurred when a balloon crash in Tullamore, County Offaly, Ireland, lit a blaze that burned down some hundred houses.

Aeronauts were only beginning to understand their craft: how to get weather and air currents to work for, not against them, how to refine methods of lift and ballast. These shocking fatalities fueled the controversy over the value and utility of ballooning. Was it just a dangerous spectacle? Would—should—balloon fever be allowed to end as swiftly as it had begun?

*The first fatal balloon crash claims Jean-François Pilâtre de Rozier and Pierre Romain near Boulogne, France, June 15, 1785.*

Novelist Horace Walpole reported in a 1785 letter, "The Balloonomania is, I think, a little chilled, not extinguished by Rozier's catastrophe."

For spectators, the perils and unpredictability of balloon flight only added to the thrill, fueling aeronauts' status as romantic heroes, godlike innovators, and adventurers.

It had been less than a year since Rozier became one of the first humans to take to the skies. Now, with Romain, he was the first to topple from them. At age thirty-one, the popular "citizen-balloonist" became a martyr to a brave new science. "It is said that perhaps he loved glory too much," one obituary opined.

Rozier's funeral was a grand, national affair, and his fiancée, after witnessing the tragedy firsthand, died just eight days later, some said of a broken heart.

➤ ◄

The same month that Rozier came crashing down to a hero's death, the first British heroine journeyed up.

Inspired by Thible's voyage in France the year before, several women in England, including the influential Georgiana, the Duchess of Devonshire, had campaigned for the honor of being the nation's first female balloon passenger, but in vain.

To many eighteenth-century minds, the idea of male balloonists soaring through the air with lady friends smacked of scandal and impropriety. The year before, London's *Morning Post* had reported that a certain Lord Cholmondeley was boasting about town of his plan to take a woman up in a balloon within the year for "an amorous adventure."

All this chatter soon had big-name émigré balloonists Jean-Pierre Blanchard, Vincent Lunardi, and Count Zambeccari competing to be the first in England to escort a lady into the clouds for promotional purposes. Many women who were eager to go up in a balloon, including a Miss Grist of Holborn, were disappointed on the day of a scheduled flight; if the craft exceeded weight limits, female passengers—like so many sandbags tossed overboard—were obliged to give up their seats.

A bawdy new dance hall tune called "The Air Balloon Fun" mocked the trend:

*But as disapointments crowd on us a-pace,*
*The lady was forc'd to alight from her place,*
*Some praising her courage, whilst others they cry'd,*
*I am sorry, dear madam, you're depriv'd of your ride.*


When "a lady"—a girl, actually, a fourteen-year-old dancer—finally took flight from English soil, she was French, and so was her pilot. Eager to keep his name on the lips of the English public after his successful Channel crossing, and always the career strategist, Jean-Pierre Blanchard had chosen the popular young entertainer to help him launch England's latest ballooning trend. Rosine Simonet, along with her sisters, had been performing on big London stages like Covent Garden and Drury Lane for years.

As Blanchard lifted off the morning of May 3, 1785, "The Lady was much frightened when the balloon first rose," reported an eyewitness, "but soon after seemed to have recovered herself; and M. Blanchard, in sight of a great number of people, saluted her." On horseback, Rosine's father galloped along for an hour under the balloon where she could see him and was there to embrace her when the balloon landed six miles away.

The papers applauded "the ingenious M. Blanchard" for his fourth "aerial experiment" in England, "with a lady."

An Englishwoman finally made it into the air on June 29, 1785, in one of Vincent Lunardi's balloons, without Lunardi in it.

A formal portrait commissioned for the occasion shows three figures in the balloon basket. But after lively negotiations, when the passengers' combined weight grounded the craft, Lunardi gallantly stepped out, leaving actress Letitia Ann Sage and her artist friend George Biggin, an amateur aviator, to fend for themselves in the upper altitudes.

Biggin and Sage flew from St. George's Fields in London before a massive crowd of some 150,000—ignoring, as the actress put it in a letter, "the discouragement so recently given, by the bursting of that *identical* balloon, and the more melancholy fate of poor Pilâtre de Rozier."

High in the clouds, the friends conducted scientific experiments, dined on ham and chicken, indulged in a glass of wine, and—perhaps in a nod to France's Élisabeth Thible and her escort—sang a duet, flying west along the River Thames. Like Thible, Sage endured a bumpy landing. The balloon wrecked a hedge on Harrow on the Hill thir-

*Portrait of Letitia Ann Sage in a balloon with Vincent Lunardi and George Biggin*

teen miles outside London and carved a strip through the middle of a ripe hayfield, enraging the farmer, who rained down abuse on the adventurers.

A party of young men and a headmaster from the nearby Harrow School quickly took up a collection to appease the farmer and lifted the heroine into the air, delivering her amid shouts and song to the local pub.

"There is no enterprise, however dangerous or difficult," reported *New London Magazine,* "but that the female mind can summon courage enough to undertake it." Sage had demonstrated "that manly fortitude which constitutes the heroine," and her flight was a sensation.

On the ground, eighteenth-century woman had very few channels for competing on equal turf with men. A woman's place was in the home. Bravery and fortitude were "manly" prerogatives.

In a letter to a friend the next day, Sage confided, "I feel myself more happy, and infinitely better pleased with my excursion than I ever was at any former event of my life."

Before long, female aeronauts would prove not only willing but able to brave life in the upper stories, paving the way for Madame Sophie Blanchard's breathtaking success a decade later.

But at the moment, back in France, political urgency had taken center stage.

*A contemporary illustration of the Women's March on Versailles, October 5, 1789*

# CHAPTER 10

# Revolution!

*1789–1799*

Sophie was eleven years old when revolution erupted in her country. She came of age against the backdrop of Revolutionary France. Was she sheltered, in her remote hamlet by the sea, from its excesses? From bloodshed?

With the vast majority of French citizens reduced to destitution before and during the struggle, her family surely suffered along with the rest. One traveler in rural France at the time wrote, "The poor seem poor indeed; the children terribly ragged, if possible worse clad than if with no clothes at all."

Revolution had been a long time coming. Two decades of drought, livestock disease, and bad harvests had turned desperate French peasants and the urban poor—artisans and laborers—against a system that very literally taxed their survival.

Bread shortages and inflated prices were salt in the wounds at a time when working people already resented their privileged king and queen, the ruling aristocracy, and the established leaders of the Catholic Church.

Louis XVI and Marie-Antoinette and their flamboyant royal court were seen as frivolous and indifferent to the needs of the people. France's costly involvement in the American Revolution and free spending by King Louis XVI had left the nation teetering on the brink of bankruptcy with no relief in sight.

Rather than go on feeding king and church and a massive war debt, the citizens of France outwardly rebelled against their feudal masters. Furious riots, looting, and strikes became the norm. As one rural mayor wrote, "The populace is so enraged they would kill for a bushel."

Beginning in 1789, sweeping change would envelop the nation for more than a decade. As the world around Sophie shifted and transformed, she had plenty of time to long for a new and bolder way of life.

A common theme in French folktales and fairy tales of the day—the sort Sophie's mother might have told while they sat side by side at the hearth squinting over needlework—was escape, whether from hunger or danger, through cunning or luck. In these tales, widows and children gathering wood in the forest elude murderous brigands with the aid of magic bracelets. Magic tablecloths unroll banquets. Girls and women yoked to plows and spinning wheels outwit tyrannical husbands, who then become princes.

Even before a brutal famine pushed feudal France to its breaking point, a young dreamer, however timid and anxious, had reason enough to fly away from reality in her thoughts.

⤖ ⤛

In May, King Louis XVI called together the *États généraux,* the Estates General, or nationwide assembly—an advisory body without real legislative power—for its first meeting since 1614, to discuss the failing economy and how, as a society, to move forward.

## The Three Estates

In France's *ancien régime,* or "old regime," which ruled from the late Middle Ages until the French Revolution of 1789, every citizen was the subject of an absolute king, with their individual rights decided by their social standing, divided into three social layers, or estates.

The first estate, and the smallest, was the clergy (those who prayed): priests, monks, bishops, nuns, and others who worked for the church.

The second estate was the nobility (those who fought for the king), made up of people with hereditary lands and wealth—another small, privileged "ratio" of the nation but with high status, political influence, and a small tax burden.

The third estate, by far the majority at roughly ninety-eight percent of the population, were the common folk of France (those who worked): peasants, craftspeople, and farm laborers who paid steep taxes and were obliged to

*A satirical cartoon of the Estates General showing Louis XVI, a bishop, and a member of the aristocracy riding on the back of a man, representing the people, who is blindfolded and in chains and crawling on his hands and knees*

77

work a certain number of days for free each year for the local lord or the king.

Each of the three estates submitted a list of demands in advance of the meeting, though they couldn't agree on how to organize a vote.

Decades later, French sociologist Alexis de Tocqueville studied these reports, or "grievance books," and was stunned:

> When I came to gather all the individual wishes, with a sense of terror I realized that their demands were for the wholesale and systematic abolition of all the laws and all the current practices in the country. Straightaway I saw that the issue here was one of the most extensive and dangerous revolutions ever observed in the world.

During the assembly, all three estates pledged loyalty to the king but suggested that absolute monarchy was obsolete.

Meetings of the Estates General should be routine, many argued, so that all the voices of France could be heard.

Taxes should be more fairly distributed among the populace.

The Church had too much power and was in dire need of reform.

Royal ministers should be held fiscally accountable.

The king should make a full disclosure of state debt and grant the Estates General control over taxation and spending.

Competing demands surfaced at the assembly, but citizens from all three estates seemed to agree: the king must be stripped of power.

The assembly spelled the beginning of the end for Louis XVI's reign.

The events that followed the historic meeting would topple the traditional foundations of French society, from the hereditary rights of the monarchy and aristocracy to the towering influence of the Catholic Church.

The Estates General was one of the first practices to go.

After a debate over how to structure a vote dragged on for days, the third estate made a bold move. On June 17, 1789, it splintered off altogether, establishing a distinct "National Assembly." Its members met on their own, inviting individuals from the other estates to join them in drafting a new vision for the country.

Louis XVI responded to the insurrection with unusual decisiveness. He ordered the building where the National Assembly was holding its meetings closed. The group convened, instead, on a tennis court at Versailles, pledging an oath to continue meeting until the king acknowledged them as a legitimate governing body and until a constitution was drafted.

## France and America

In 1777, at age nineteen, the idealistic young French aristocrat the Marquis de Lafayette defied a direct order from King Louis XVI, paying his own way to cross the Atlantic and join up with the struggling American Continental Army. Though he had served in the French military, Lafayette had no battle experience when he reached the New World, but the young major general fast distinguished himself and was warmly embraced by commander in chief George Washington.

When revolution swept through France a decade later, prominent Americans threw their support behind the wave of change just as educated French citizens like Lafayette, inspired by

Enlightenment ideals of freedom, liberty, and justice for all, had supported America's struggle.

In 1789, United States Founding Father Thomas Jefferson was serving as minister to France. Recognized around the world as the author of the Declaration of Independence, he had the ear of French revolutionaries. His host nation had been inspired by the American Revolution, he claimed, and he offered his home as a meeting place for rebels aligned with Lafayette, who had returned to France in 1782.

*The first meeting of George Washington and the Marquis de Lafayette, 1777*

Leaders like Lafayette had come home with firsthand experience of the principles and practices of the American struggle and put them to work during negotiations with Louis XVI and the evolving revolutionary government.

After the historic storming of the Bastille in July 1789, which signaled the start of the revolution, Lafayette was named commander in chief of France's National Guard and attempted to steer a middle course through the volatile years to come. Despite his progressive ideals, he was a member of the aristocracy and continued to support the king and the idea of a constitutional monarchy, a shared system of government anchored by a constitution.

Together with clergyman Abbé Sieyès, and in consultation with Thomas Jefferson, Lafayette would draft France's "The Declaration of the Rights of Man and of the Citizen," a summary of the values of the French Revolution. The document, like America's Declaration of Independence, listed rights and freedoms, ostensibly for all, and was adopted by the new government or National Assembly that August.

By July 14, when enraged Parisian mobs stormed the fortress prison of the Bastille, a cruel symbol of the absolute and unjust rule, the revolution was in full swing. Louis XVI, meanwhile, spoke of reform but resisted it, and on October 5, 1789, enraged citizens (led by women fed up with sky-high bread prices, bread shortages, and grain riots) along with some fifteen thousand National Guardsmen (led by the Marquis de Lafayette and working to control the fray) marched twelve rainy miles from Paris to Versailles to confront the king and his despised queen.

The mob arrived in a mud-splattered fury with women brandishing kitchen knives, brooms, and pikes.

*A portrait of King Louis XVI of France, circa 1779, by Antoine-François Callet*

Rushing the palace gates, the crowd forced its way through, screaming and singing and howling invectives at Queen Marie-Antoinette, who cowered under guard in her bedchamber. The people demanded bread. They ordered the sheltered nobles to move to Paris and serve their subjects. By the following day, the royal family had complied.

Refusing to formally give up his duties as king over the next year and a half, Louis made a risky attempt to escape to Austria with his family in June 1791 amid swirling rumors of treason. He and the queen were apprehended and brought back under guard. The following year, they were arrested and imprisoned.

In September 1792, the French National Convention (a new name for the National Assembly) charged the king with treason and abolished the monarchy, declaring France a Republic to be governed by a revised assembly called the Convention.

## Eye in the Sky

The abolition of the monarchy in France triggered the French Revolutionary Wars, a series of military conflicts lasting from 1792 until 1802, with the French Republic targeting countries governed at the time by monarchies, including Great Britain, Holland, Austria, Prussia, Russia, and Spain.

The French military, meanwhile, ushered in the age of military aircraft. During the Battle of Fleurus on June 26, 1794, the army sent up a tethered hydrogen balloon, *l'Entreprenant,* to track the movements of the Austrian Army.

It wasn't exactly the scenario Benjamin Franklin had envisioned years before—thousands of balloons transporting "troops rapidly into the field, crossing rivers, hills or even seas with speed and impunity"—but it was a novelty, a menacing eye in the sky that

*The June 26, 1794, Battle of Fleurus*
*with the observation balloon* l'Entreprenant *overhead*

unnerved the enemy on the ground and triggered fearful rumors of aerial invasion among the Austrian soldiers.

The reconnaissance balloon stayed up in the air for nine hours while two members of the fledgling French Aerostatic Corps took notes on the movements of the Austrian Army. The two corpsmen waved signal flags, dropped intel to the ground, or anchored messages in sandbags they slid down long mooring ropes on metal rings for French soldiers to collect.

On January 21, 1793, convicted and condemned, Louis XVI was led to the guillotine. Marie-Antoinette was executed the same way in October. The couple's young son died in prison, though their daughter would be released to family in Austria.

Fearing they might lose their own lives, as some thousand royalists and suspected traitors to revolution had the previous fall—condemned and executed by mock courts nationwide during the "September massacres"—thousands of aristocrats and French military officers began to flee France.

The Reign of Terror was on, spearheaded by radical leader Maximilien Robespierre, who had successfully lobbied for the king's death sentence and now urged the people to send any and all enemies of the Revolution to the guillotine.

Before the Terror ended with Robespierre's death—by guillotine—in July 1794, a span of less than a year, about 300,000 suspects were arrested and some 17,000 executed. Some 10,000 more would die in prison or otherwise never see trial.

Women in France played an active role throughout the Revolution (which officially ended in 1799), particularly those—like the women who marched on Versailles—whose families faced extreme poverty and deprivation. Women were also active counterrevolutionaries, defending their religion and traditional way of life. In the loyalist Catholic region known as the Vendée, north of Sophie's home, many women resented revolutionary intrusion into religious matters and defended the Church and its priests, who were under siege by a radical new government.

Given her apolitical behavior as an adult, it's hard to imagine teenage Sophie dancing around a Liberty Tree (a popular symbol of the new political freedom) in a revolutionary red bonnet. But the unsettled state of her country certainly would have mirrored any restlessness she felt in adolescence, feeding dreams of freedom or escape or both—perhaps even in a balloon, high above the earth.

SIC ITUR AD ASTRA

45.ᵗʰ Aſcenſion and the firſt made in America January 9.ᵗʰ 1793. at Philadelphia 39.56ʹ N. Latitude by Mr. J.P. Blanchard.

45.ᵉ aſcenſion et la premiere faite en Amerique Le 9 Janvier 1793 a Philadelphie 39.56 Latitude N. par Mr. J.P. Blanchard.

JOURNAL

OF MY

FORTY-FIFTH

ASCENSION,

BEING THE FIRST PERFORMED IN

AMERICA,

ON THE NINTH OF JANUARY, 1793.

*Æthereum tranabit iter, quo numine* BLANCHARD?
*Impavidus, fortem non timet Icariam.*

PHILADELPHIA:

PRINTED BY CHARLES CIST, No. 104. NORTH
SECOND-STREET, M,DCC,XCIII.

Title page of Jean-Pierre Blanchard's published account
of his 1793 flight in Philadelphia

# CHAPTER 11

# Star-Spangled Voyager

Jean-Pierre Blanchard flies in America
*Philadelphia; January 9, 1793*

Sophie's future husband fled the chaos of both the revolution in their homeland and impending war between France and England by taking his one-man air show on the road again. After forty-four acclaimed flights in Europe, many of them "firsts," he now hoped to be the first person to fly in America.

On September 30, 1792, he sailed from England aboard the ship *Ceres,* docking in Philadelphia in December. He would make his forty-fifth ascent in the city that was, at the time, the capital of a bold young United States and the permanent home of Benjamin Franklin, President George Washington, and many prominent American revolutionaries.

As it turned out, Blanchard would not be the first person to float up from American soil. That honor had been quietly claimed eight years earlier by a lawyer and tavern keeper named Peter Carnes, who read about the Montgolfiers and was inspired to build his own small hot-air balloon—and by a brave thirteen-year-old boy named Edward Warren, who had volunteered to go up in it. But if Blanchard was disappointed, he didn't let on.

No sooner had President Washington and Pennsylvania's governor general, Thomas Mifflin, received him than the French showman set his publicity machine churning. For several weeks, to finance the flight—and make a profit, he hoped—Blanchard ran an ad in *Dunlap's American Daily Advertiser* stating that he would fly a hydrogen or "inflammable gas" balloon from Walnut Street Prison yard on January 9, 1793, at ten in the morning, weather permitting, and offered public subscriptions at a hefty $5 (about $135 today).

He had "the desire of beholding you in the full enjoyment of the blessings of liberty," Blanchard told his American readers, "under the protection of your newly established government." He pledged to show "the New World that man's ingenuity is not confined to earth alone, but opens to him new and certain roads in the vast expanse of heaven."

## From Country to Country on the Wings of the Wind

By the time Blanchard made his historic ascent from Philadelphia's Walnut Street Prison yard in 1793, America was already well acquainted with the balloon.

Three influential Americans—Benjamin Franklin, John Adams, and John Jay—had been in Paris negotiating for an end to the American Revolutionary War when the first balloon flights took place in 1783. These diplomats saw the launches firsthand and regularly reported home. In a letter to a U.S. congressman, Jay had proposed that "travelers may hereafter literally pass from country to country on the wings of the wind," and Franklin reported regularly on balloons and balloonomania in letters to family, friends, and colleagues.

American newspapers began to cover balloon activity as early as November 1783, and on both sides of the Atlantic people hailed the miraculous globes as signs of a new era, when science and technology would change everything, reflecting revolutionary principles of liberty, equality, and justice.

When he arrived in Philadelphia in 1792, to great fanfare, Blanchard put the rhetoric of progress and revolution to work in his promotional materials.

*Portrait of Benjamin Franklin circa 1793, by Pierre-Michel Alix*

As in Europe, many adventurers clamored to go with Blanchard, but as usual, the aeronaut had no intention of sharing the glory if it could be helped. In a notice in the *Federal Gazette,* he cautioned the curious not to follow him on horseback: "Permit me, gentlemen, to advise you not to attempt to keep up with me, especially in a country so intersected with rivers, and so covered with woods." The balloonist did consent to conduct a handful of scientific experiments in the air.

By dawn on the day of the ascent, most of the residents of the city and many travelers had formed a teeming crowd. The excitement in and beyond the Walnut Street Prison yard was palpable.

Blanchard had been at the balloon site since about four that morning, leaving his lodgings on North Eighth Street nearly in time to watch the waning crescent moon rise. It was just below freezing out, and the sky was "serene," he recalled later, "spangled with ten thousand glittering stars."

When he recorded the temperature at 6 a.m. it was a balmy thirty degrees Fahrenheit. Two field cannons began firing from a nearby burial ground every fifteen minutes, calling citizens to witness the miraculous voyage of a hydrogen balloon from American soil.

By 8 a.m., the temperature had risen to thirty-five degrees. The sky was "overcast and hazy." Clouds or no clouds, Blanchard filled the balloon with hydrogen. Serenaded by a brass band as he worked, he stocked the gondola with food, wine, and scientific instruments. At some point, an excited onlooker rushed forward with a little black dog, pushing it into Blanchard's arms, and the dubious pilot dropped his passenger into the basket.

Decked out in a royal-blue waistcoat and knee breeches, topped by a hat with a white feather, Blanchard circled the gradually expanding bag of yellow silk, making adjustments.

At quarter to ten, President Washington arrived by carriage. Fifteen cannons sounded a salute, and the milling crowd oohed and aahed as he stepped down. A solemn hush followed as the dignitary and his entourage settled in for the show. Future presidents John Adams, Thomas Jefferson—who had returned from France in 1789—James Madison, and James Monroe were also in the audience.

By ten, it was a fair day with a light breeze. The sun shone in a clear sky. The petite aeronaut strutted out, chatted with the president, the French ambassador, and other notables, one reporter noted, then "leap'd into his boat which was painted blue and spangled" and lifted off from the interior prison yard.

More cannon fire marked the moment. Blanchard threw out some ballast and signaled two assistants to let go of the ropes. The wicker basket shot upward under the bright yellow globe.

"When [the balloon] began to rise," went one report, "the majestical sight was truly awful and interesting. . . . Indeed the attention of the multitude was so absorbed that it was a considerable time e'er silence was broke."

The crowd gasped as Blanchard careened overhead, waving his hat in one hand and a flag "ornamented on one side with the armoric bearings of the United States, and on the other with the three colors so dear to the French nation" in the other.

"Seeing the man waving a flag at an immense height from the ground," wrote a spectator, "was the most interesting sight that I ever beheld, and tho I had no acquaintance with him, I could not help trembling for his safety."

To Blanchard, people seemed to cover every open space below, "the roofs of the houses, the steeples, the streets, and the roads."

Around 10:10 a.m., the wind steered the balloon to the southeast. "Several Gentlemen gallop'd down the point road," Blanchard noted, "but soon lost sight of it, for it moved at a rate of 20 miles an hour."

"For a long time," he wrote, "could I hear the cries of joy."

A surge of wind whisked the balloon toward the Delaware River, parting a flock of startled wild pigeons. Blanchard's canine companion whimpered at the thunder of wings, and he calmed her with a pat on the head. The sparkling river below seemed to him a ribbon "about four inches" wide.

The flight topped off at 5,812 feet, per Blanchard's barometric measurements, and as promised, he emptied bottles of "divers liquors" to collect air samples under a hermetic seal, took his pulse rate to compare it to the rate on solid ground (ninety-two beats per minute, eight beats more), and judged the magnetic properties of a lodestone (1.5 ounces less at highest altitude than on the ground).

After dashing off notes on air pressure, temperature, and weather conditions, he fortified himself with "a morsel of biscuit and a glass of wine" until the wind reared up, and it was time to ready for landing on the New Jersey side of the Delaware River.

Stowing his instruments and supplies, he emptied ballast, opened the hydrogen valve, and began his descent, skidding down into a stripped field near Woodbury, New Jersey, at around 10:56.

The balloon had soared fifteen miles in forty-six minutes.

The moment his furry copilot had all four legs on the ground, she ran for the nearest tree and then lapped water from a pond.

Blanchard set to work deflating the balloon so it wouldn't billow into a nearby cluster of trees, unloading and inspecting his gear as a wary farmer approached. Blanchard always needed help packing up at this stage and called to the stunned fellow in French, tempting him closer with a bottle of wine. The farmer accepted a swallow, and thanks to the "exhilarating juice of the grape," Blanchard had an enthusiastic assistant. The farmer was illiterate and couldn't read the passport Blanchard showed him, but he recognized Washington's name.

Another man approached with a rifle but soon dropped his weapon and "lifted up his hands toward heaven."

## A Presidential Passport

A fan of new technologies, the American president George Washington knew of the fever for balloon experiments that had overtaken Europe. Like many Americans, he was fascinated with these overseas reports, writing to a friend in April 1784, "I have only news paper accts. of Air Balloons, to which I do not know what credence to give. The tales related of them are marvelous, and lead us to expect that our friends at Paris, in a little time, will come flying thro' the air, instead of ploughing the ocean to get to America."

In another letter dated more than a year later, he recommended that "young men of science and spirit" should be offered "handsome public encouragements . . . for the risks they run in ascertaining its [the balloon's] usefulness."

When Blanchard arrived, Washington not only welcomed him and attended his launch, he provided a "passport" or letter of introduction. The showman still spoke little English, despite his time in England, and the letter—the first airmail delivery in America—would guarantee him safe passage upon landing.

> *George Washington, President of the United States of America, to all to whom these presents shall come. The bearer hereof, Mr. Blanchard a citizen of France, proposing to ascend in a balloon from the city of Philadelphia, at 10 o'clock, A. M. this day, to pass in such direction and to descend in such place as circumstances may render most convenient—These are therefore to recommend to all citizens of the United States, and others, that in his passage, descent, return or journeying elsewhere, they oppose no hindrance or molestation to the said Mr. Blanchard; And, that on the contrary, they receive and aid him with that humanity and good will which may render honor to their country, and justice to an individual so distinguished by his efforts to establish and advance an art, in order to make it useful to mankind in general.*

As others arrived, Blanchard circulated the passport and the wine, and the newcomers read "in the midst of a profound silence. . . . How dear the name Washington is to this people!" Blanchard recorded. "With what eagerness they gave me all possible assistance, in consequence of his recommendation!"

Before Blanchard and his wagonload of balloon paraphernalia embarked for Philadelphia, he scribbled out a certificate of landing: "[W]e the subscribers saw the bearer, Mr. Blanchard, settle in his balloon in Deptford Township, County of Gloucester, in the State of New Jersey . . . about 10 o'clock 56 minutes, A.M. . . . the ninth day of January, Anno Domini, 1793," and asked his assistants to sign.

By seven that evening, he was back in Philadelphia, with fans lined up to shake his hand. To their hushed delight, Blanchard offered the American president the flag he had flown during his flight.

"For some time days past the conversation in our city has turned wholly upon Mr. Blanchard's late Aerial Voyage," one doctor wrote afterward to a colleague. "It was truly a sublime sight. Every faculty of the mind was seized, expanded and captivated by it, 40,000 people concentrating their eyes and thoughts at the *same* instant, upon the *same* object, and all deriving nearly the *same* degree of pleasure from it."

Blanchard won glory that day but little financial gain. It would be a theme in his life. The $405 he earned from ticket sales—plus an additional $263 in donations—was no match for the $1,500 in expenses he had racked up.

After failed moneymaking schemes on the ground in Philadelphia, Boston, South Carolina, and New York, Blanchard sailed back to France in the spring of 1797. That August, he returned to the clouds, likely for the first time in four years. But a little-attended flight in Nantes left him so angry that he threatened to quit the business altogether. "I therefore make an end here of my ascents," he sniffed, offering his aerial equipment for sale in a classified ad. "These dismembered balloons will make excellent cloaks, caps, aprons, and umbrellas."

Somehow the pioneering—if petulant—balloonist found the encouragement and heart to keep going. And soon, he would have a partner in his high-flying exploits.

*Portrait of Napoléon Bonaparte, circa 1805, by Jacques-Louis David*

# CHAPTER 12

# A New Emperor and
# the First Family of the Clouds

The Rise of Napoléon; The Fall of Garnerin

*1796–1804*

With France's bloody Reign of Terror at an end, Napoléon Bonaparte, an ambitious young general who had been rising quietly—or not so quietly—through the ranks of the French military during the Revolution, squashed an October 1795 rebellion against the new government by royalists loyal to the old monarchy. Hailed as a hero, Napoléon was appointed commander in chief of the French army on March 2, 1796.

Seven days later, he married the equally ambitious Joséphine de Beauharnais.

Just over three years later, in a November 1799 coup d'état, Napoléon would seize absolute power and create a vast empire from the rubble of the French Revolution.

A shrewd military strategist, he expanded his domain by waging war on several fronts and restoring order in France by reconciling old ways and new, allowing many exiled aristocrats to return and restoring the Catholic Church to prominence.

By 1804, he had crowned himself emperor and Joséphine empress.

➤ ◄

While Blanchard, Lunardi, and others of the older generation of superstar balloonists had slowed down during the Revolution or worked outside war-torn France and England, a new aeronaut-showman had emerged on the scene.

On October 22, 1797, twenty-seven-year-old André-Jacques Garnerin took the first recorded parachute jump from a balloon—from around three thousand feet—over Parc Monceau, a public park in Paris. In what was at the time a thrilling feat, he detached his hydrogen balloon from its gondola and let the balloon sail off as the frameless silk parachute he'd invented billowed out above him.

## Taking the Leap

Parachute designs had been kicking around for some two hundred years when Frenchman Louis-Sébastien Lenormand was credited with inventing the modern parachute and making the first recorded jump in 1783. Early chutes were made of linen stretched over a wooden frame. Jean-Pierre Blanchard introduced folded silk into the equation in the late 1790s for a stronger, lighter model, and sent a dog up as test passenger. In 1793, he himself, in a stroke of poetic justice, became the first to parachute from a balloon—not by choice—when his balloon envelope burst.

Garnerin had studied physics but began developing balloon designs along with ideas for putting the craft to military use. When

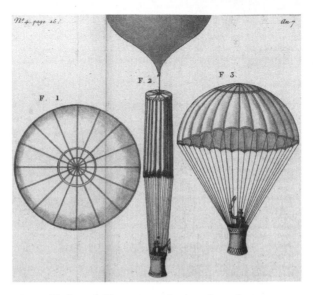

*Technical illustration of a parachute design*
*by André-Jacques Garnerin, around 1800*

revolution broke out, he joined the French army, was captured during the conflict with England, and was imprisoned in a Hungarian castle.

For three long years, the balloonist dreamed of fleeing the castle's stone courtyard in the basket of a balloon or of leaping from the high battlement walls below a parachute. Though Garnerin didn't escape or get the chance to test his innovations in Hungary, he would go on to invent—and demonstrate—the first "frameless" silk parachute.

Garnerin would prove to be a savvy professional showman, the first to turn the standard balloon launch into a full-on circus with acrobatic displays, parachute drops, night flights, and fireworks. A year after his parachuting debut, in 1798, the showman reworked the old stunt of bringing a lady companion up into the air. The young woman, billed as Citoyenne ("Citizen") Henri, would be the first of her sex brave enough to take to the skies, he claimed (failing to credit Élisabeth Thible or Letitia Ann Sage).

The war-weary French public and press were all for a racy drama. But the Central Bureau of Police called Garnerin in to defend his morally suspect mission. The balloonist took full responsibility for his charge's safety and well-being, but the Bureau slapped an injunction on him. The Minister of Interior and Police overturned it. There "was no more scandal in seeing two people of different sexes ascend in a balloon," he argued, "than it is to see them jump into a carriage." What's more, the intrepid female had the utmost confidence in the experiment.

Garnerin went to work advertising the launch, reporting in *L'Ami des Lois:* "The young citoyenne who will accompany me is delighted to see the day approach for the journey . . . some time during the next ten days."

On July 8, 1798, a crowd gathered to watch the pair fly off without incident. They landed about nineteen miles north of Paris, after which the ornamental young passenger became, like Thible before her, a footnote in the history of aerostation.

On the other hand, Jeanne-Geneviève Labrosse, who eventually became Garnerin's wife and business partner, would prove to be anything but a footnote. Together with her husband and their daredevil niece Élisa, Labrosse headlined a celebrated family act.

# The Aerial Exploits of
# Jeanne-Geneviève Labrosse Garnerin

At the age of twenty-two, Jeanne-Geneviève Labrosse was in the crowd when André-Jacques Garnerin made his historic balloon ascent—and descent by parachute—over Paris in October of 1797.

When the balloonist returned, slightly battered, to earth, the young would-be aeronaut introduced herself. Labrosse would go on to become one of Garnerin's star students. Soon after, the two would marry and form a business partnership.

On November 10, 1798, Labrosse claimed fame as the first woman to fly solo in a balloon. The following year, she found fame as the first woman to parachute from one—at an altitude of 2,953 feet.

The Garnerins caused a stir three years later when, during a publicity stunt in England, they put Jeanne's cat to work as a skydiver. One newspaper reported: "This evening Mr. and Mrs. Garnerin . . . ascended from Vauxhall in a balloon," rising to six thousand feet and enlisting the poor animal to come "down from this stupendous height in a parachute with perfect safety" in a basket.

*French fashion magazine illustration of high-society spectators watching
Jeanne-Geneviève Garnerin fly in a balloon on March 28, 1802*

To quell the public outcry that followed, the Garnerins sent a letter to the press from "Tom Cat of Poland Street": "Brought up under the care of Madame Garnerin, I may be said to have been nursed in the very bosom of aerostation," the captive hero reported, and was therefore "determined on sharing the danger of her new voyage." Share he did, as his human dropped him overboard in a basket strapped to a parachute:

> *Every eye was turned from the balloon and fixed upon me, and several ladies swooned, fearing I should fall into the river. . . . You have no idea of the crowds that ran from all sides to offer me their assistance. They rushed with so much impetuosity that they tumbled over one another into the ditches.*

A crowd of hundreds rescued the feline diver and escorted him home to the address on his collar. They also tore the Garnerins' parachute to bits, "to prevent me from ever exposing myself to a similar danger."

Tom's public plight notwithstanding, the Garnerin show went on. The celebrity couple, and hapless pets, toured all over Europe to great acclaim with Jeanne boldly parachuting from altitudes up to eight thousand feet.

The Garnerins built their image as the glamorous and fearless first family of aerial entertainment, drawing huge crowds wherever they went.

Napoléon had kept a close eye on ballooning both for its military potential and for its role in propaganda and public relations. Well aware

*André-Jacques and Jeanne-Geneviève Garnerin*

of the success of Garnerin and his family, he wasted no time in naming the airman his "Official Aeronaut of France."

With his imperial position established, Napoléon now needed to manage his image, and what better way to create a patriotic stir in Paris than with a balloon? He commissioned Garnerin to build and launch an enormous unpiloted celebration balloon to mark his coronation as emperor.

Napoléon and Joséphine would devote the day following their lavish and solemn ceremony at Notre-Dame Cathedral to "a programme of games and races resembling those of antiquity" in a huge circus arena.

On December 3, 1804, Garnerin launched his balloon from the front of Notre-Dame with flags, banners, and drapes flapping. Suspended from its hoop on golden chains were three thousand lights shaped to form an imperial crown.

But it is no easy feat to plan around a balloon.

About forty-six hours later, according to Italian reports, Garnerin's creation splashed down on Lake Bracciano near Rome. Some claimed to have seen the rogue balloon *in* the imperial city. It sailed toward the Vatican and low across the Forum, snagging forebodingly on the stone of an ancient tomb, a piece of which broke off as the rogue bobbed away over the Pontine Marshes. The broken tomb belonged to none other than the murderous Roman emperor Nero.

The newly crowned Napoléon did not, to put it lightly, enjoy the association, or the jokes it inspired. The balloon mishap was a bad omen that linked his coronation as emperor to an imperial tyrant. It was an embarrassment to the crown.

From there, the emperor soured for a time on the whole business of ballooning, leaving Garnerin and his marvelous feats out of royal favor and throwing a wrench into a thriving family business.

The brave Garnerin women had ushered in a golden age of female flight, but they were about to be eclipsed.

*French balloonist Marie Madeleine-Sophie Armant Blanchard,*
*early 1800s*

# CHAPTER 13

# Incomparable Sensation!

Sophie Marries Jean-Pierre and Becomes an Aeronaut
*1804–1809*

The same month and year that André-Jacques Garnerin so dramatically disappointed his emperor, Sophie Armant went up for the first time in a balloon.

Was her pilot, by then, her husband? How and when did they meet?

Most likely, the couple invented the story of the balloonist's crash landing in the coastal village of Trois-Canons—along with Blanchard's pledge to the innkeepers to return sixteen years later and claim the hand of their unborn daughter in marriage. It was a good story, the stuff of legend, and it made for even better publicity.

But in fact, Sophie was born in March 1778, five years before recorded human flight. Since the story features Jean-Pierre falling from the sky (and he wasn't exactly the sort to keep a historic achievement like "first human in the air" a secret), the dates don't match up.

Perhaps he did crash in the meadow near the family inn, but many years after Sophie's birth. Perhaps he fell from the sky when she was a teen, and they met, and it was love at first sight. Or perhaps she traveled to one of his launches and overcame her paralyzing shyness long enough to strike up a conversation. They could have met in countless ways, but one thing we know: Jean-Pierre Blanchard took Sophie Armant up in an air balloon over Marseille in 1804 and won her heart.

Accounts vary, but she was between sixteen and twenty-six when they married. Blanchard had long since abandoned his first wife, Victoire Lebrun, and their children to chase ballooning fame. He was decades older than his second bride.

Who was Sophie when he invited her up into the air? A young woman hungry, no doubt, for freedom and adventure, if perhaps too petrified to seek it. People described her as "birdlike" and eccentric. Tiny with large eyes and timid to the point of awkwardness, she panicked around crowds, horses, and loud noises. Hardly aeronaut material.

But on that first balloon ride over Marseille, Sophie broke her typical excruciating silence to look down and cry out, *"Sensation incomparable!"*

What Sophie may not have known was that her soon-to-be husband was flat broke, on the brink of bankruptcy. No longer a young man, Blanchard was running out of time to ballast his sinking career. He was well aware of the success of the Garnerin family, at least before its patriarch fell out of favor with Napoléon; and as André-Jacques Garnerin and Citizen Henri had proved, women in the air were still a novelty. The stakes seemed higher for female passengers and balloonists at a time when society still cast women as frail and vulnerable, with "delicate" constitutions. A damsel in distress—or the hint of scandal when male and female balloonists like George Biggin and Letitia Ann Sage braved the ether alone together—drew eager crowds.

But the daring Garnerin women, who were performing aerial stunts few men could match, were the furthest thing from damsels in distress. The publicity-savvy first family of the clouds had paved the way for bold women aeronauts, and Blanchard knew just how to display Sophie to best advantage to drum up new audiences.

Ever the opportunist, he took his new bride as his protégée, and soon Sophie was his fearless ballooning partner as well as his wife.

She took to her new role and its costume—a glamorous white gown—with gusto, and while at first her supporting role was limited, the pupil was eager. Sophie quickly displayed acrobatic grace and a sure instinct for controlling a balloon.

Publicly, Sophie's main rival in the air was Élisa Garnerin, who, like her famous aunt and uncle, not only flew balloons but parachuted out of them, to the astonishment of audiences all over Europe.

## Sophie's Nemesis

André-Jacques Garnerin's niece learned to fly balloons at age fifteen. In September 1815, during her first parachute drop at the Jardin du Tivoli in Paris before the king of Prussia and his son, a violent wind set her parachute spinning. One reporter wrote that she managed the descent "majestically and without danger." But in fact, danger was Élisa Garnerin's middle name, and she would make thirty-nine such leaps between 1815 and 1836 in Italy, Spain, Russia, and Germany as well as France.

At an August 1816 festival in Paris, one also featuring a performance

*Portrait of French balloonist and parachutist Élisa Garnerin, 1791*

*Advertisement for one of Élisa Garnerin's parachute performances*

by her upstart rival, Sophie Blanchard, Élisa's advance publicity promised that she and her sister (new to ballooning) would float overhead while Élisa strummed a harp and sang the royal family's praises. Things didn't quite work out that way, as the balloon failed to lift off after three tries, forcing her sister to hop out so that Élisa could placate a crowd that had grown "seriously angry." Her flight lasted barely fifteen minutes.

During another ascent, on June 28, 1818, from Bordeaux, France, fierce winds drove her balloon south toward the harbor. When she released the balloon and activated her parachute, the crowd following along below gasped as the wind spirited her out over the river. Élisa, who couldn't swim, crashed down in the water in a tangle of parachute. Luckily two nearby boats performed a rescue. "She was very much terrified," reported one eyewitness, "when the boats came to her assistance."

Élisa and her equally intrepid aunt were beloved by the masses but until Napoléon's eventual defeat at Waterloo would struggle to find sponsorship. André-Jacques Garnerin's embarrassment of the emperor had left a stain on the family name that was hard to lift. As Sophie became better known, she would take advantage of the opening.

Sophie didn't do parachute descents like the Garnerin women, but she and Jean-Pierre experimented with the technology, and Sophie used chutes to launch increasingly impressive aerial fireworks.

For the next few years, she proved an able assistant at her husband's launches throughout Europe and North America, and at last, in June 1805, she had her chance to fly alone.

➤ ◄

Sophie's first solo flight, in the South of France near Montpellier, was an accident. Jean-Pierre Blanchard's launch had been teased and delayed several times. When the date was finally announced and the crowd gathered at Place du Peyrou, they were surprised to see Sophie step aboard the basket without her husband. She gave his apologies—the aeronaut was ill—and kept his promise to entertain them in the air.

"[The balloon's] movement at first was slow," wrote one reporter, "but when it ascended to about six hundred feet, she then threw out some ballast, and we soon lost sight of her, being confounded with the clouds, at nine or ten thousand feet of elevation, like them carried by a south-east wind towards our mountains."

Lightly clothed when she set out, Sophie met with snow and intense cold as she went higher. Even the clear sunshine above the clouds didn't warm her, and hail began to pummel her skin. Though it felt as if the balloon had leveled out, she understood she was still rising, because of the acute pain in her ear, a pulsing in the artery of her eye, and her difficulty breathing. This and the stabbing cold persuaded her to draw the cord of the valve to lower the balloon.

Soon, "with encreased happiness," she saw "the earth, the mountains, and the woods, for she thought she had been carried towards the sea." Sophie had forgotten her watch and drifted, oblivious to the time. Her audience, "who had lost sight of her, saw her again with delight, descending slowly towards the north."

After a peaceful landing, "some peasants arrived, and with much kindness assisted her."

➤ ◄

A landing two years later in Rotterdam, the Netherlands, was anything but peaceful. Their balloon snagged in a tree on the way up and was torn, forcing Sophie and Jean-Pierre to leap out of the balloon to avoid a crash. While "no fatal consequences were apprehended," reported the *Tyne Mercury,* Jean-Pierre suffered a "violent contusion on the head, particularly on one ear." Sophie showed no injuries beyond "the effect the alarm had on her mind." Very likely in shock, she was unable to speak for an undisclosed period of time. But even as her aging husband began to slow down, Sophie lost no time returning to her livelihood in the skies.

The next year, Jean-Pierre suffered a heart attack while landing a damaged balloon over The Hague in the Netherlands. He toppled out of the basket, falling more than fifty feet, and this time would not recover from his injuries.

*Scientific American* reported, in February 1808, that Sophie "stood by him during the thirteen long months that he lay paralyzed and unable to help himself." The bedridden airman confessed to his wife, "My poor dear, when I am dead I fear you will have no other resources but to throw yourself into the water."

*Jean-Pierre and Sophie Blanchard jump
to safety to avoid a crash landing, 1807.*

After three years of flights—successful and otherwise—thirty-year-old Sophie was a skilled and commanding pilot in her own right. But despite her contributions to the business, her partner's money-management skills hadn't improved over the years. When Jean-Pierre died in March 1809, at age fifty-five, Sophie faced crushing debt.

The "birdlike" widow made a choice and "valiantly took up the career of him she had lost."

*Sophie Blanchard standing in the decorated basket of her balloon during her flight in Milan, Italy, in 1811*

# CHAPTER 14

# Storms and Tempests

"Aeronaut of the Official Festivals";
"Official Aeronaut of the Restoration"
*1808–1819*

Around 1819, a Dutch poet named Willem Bilderdijk wrote about a voyage he took with his wife through France. They were passengers on a public diligence, or stagecoach. No sooner did the "heavy machine begin to move," he recalled, than a lady passenger "began to scream" with "the most absurd degree of terror."

When the stagecoach reached Brussels, the woman was so "overcome that she announced her intention of stopping some days in that city to recruit her strength before venturing again to encounter the perils of a diligence."

After their fellow passenger left, the poet and his wife had a good laugh at her expense.

It wasn't until they arrived in Paris, and Bilderdijk found himself in a "tête-à-tête with the silly, frightened lady, whose nervous tremors in the Brussels diligence had afforded so much amusement to him and his wife," that he learned the identity of the hysterical traveler. She was none other than high-flying ballooning legend Sophie Blanchard.

➤ ◄

Sophie was born to fly.

In the air, she was calm, confident, light, deft, and mysteriously fearless—brave to the point of recklessness—with a knack for provoking and pleasing her audience. She was the very opposite of the jittery wallflower she was on land.

Almost immediately after Jean-Pierre's death, in January 1810, Sophie gave her first major solo balloon display in Paris. Like her rivals the Garnerins, she specialized in night flights and fireworks, but Sophie's were deliberately more brash, more daring. She had to vie with ballooning's first family for recognition, and her efforts paid off when she caught the eye of the emperor Napoléon.

Taken by her courage and bravado, Napoléon swapped Sophie in for Garnerin, naming her *Aeronaute des Fêtes Officielles,* or "Aeronaut of the Official Festivals," with formal responsibility for organizing balloon displays at all major Paris events.

Napoléon had divorced Joséphine when she couldn't give him a son and heir, and it was time to remarry. Later that summer, he would wed the Archduchess Marie-Louise of Austria, and he hired Sophie to pilot a balloon at the Imperial Royal Guard marriage celebration.

From then on, Sophie not only flew for her emperor, she was expected to act as a member of his imperial court, with entertaining as well as aerial duties.

Like Louis XVI and Marie-Antoinette's royal court before him—somewhat ironically, given that he'd aided the Revolution in deposing a privileged monarchy—Napoléon's was a lavish hive of fuss and fashion. Though he had seized absolute power through military genius,

Napoléon was not from a noble or royal background. He was an ambitious general from Corsica. The Revolution had given him power, but now he had to look the part of a respected leader as well as fight like one.

After establishing his guard and settling into the royal palace, the status-conscious Napoléon held weekly receptions. His courtiers—many former revolutionaries who claimed to despise the monarchy and live only for the Republic—ended up dressing and behaving like their former oppressors.

They were expected to wear silk stockings and buckled shoes, sashes, cloaks, and feathered hats, and to follow formal etiquette. He had some three thousand servants and attendants in his household, compared to Louis's two thousand or so.

Napoléon was a brusque, at times rude ruler, who lashed out in conversation with the same strategic aggression he displayed on the battlefield. Napoléon did not like to be disappointed, and despite her jumpiness and unease on land, Sophie did not disappoint.

For the sake of getting into and staying in the air, she rose to the challenges at court, styling herself as none had done before in high-waisted dresses of white cotton—long-sleeved to cover her knuckles and warm her hands in chilly upper altitudes—and showy white bonnets with ostrich plumes to make her more visible in her airy element.

She also honed her ballooning style, doing away with Jean-Pierre's big, battered balloon canopy with its ponderous basket. Instead, she had a small silk balloon made with a tiny open gondola barely three feet long and a foot high on the edges, which only reached her knees while she was standing. The gondola was outfitted with a little upholstered armchair for her to sit or sleep in (to escape her stress and worry on land, she often went up alone, enjoying the peaceful silence of the night skies in the place where she felt the safest).

The silver, cradle-shaped gondola offered little buffer between her and the wild wind.

As she gripped her balloon ropes, Sophie was almost literally one with the clouds. From the ground, she must have looked fragile as well as fearless—a contradiction she cultivated in her performances, which were increasingly in demand around Europe.

> ↤

In September 1810, slated for a much-publicized show in Frankfurt, Germany, Sophie realized that her ship was leaking hydrogen and would soon be unable to rise. Crowds were always restless at balloon launches, fearful of being disappointed by one of the many possible technical glitches. Thinking quickly, Sophie removed the gondola to lighten her craft, positioned herself gracefully on the narrow ring fastened to the balloon's netting, and sailed aloft to great fanfare. Lightly balanced on her hoop, she soared over the heads of her dazzled audience and across the River Main. She managed to stay aloft for a good two hours, traversing about twenty-five miles, until the cold forced her to land.

When Napoléon and Marie-Louise's son was born on March 20, 1811, Sophie flew from Champ de Mars, scattering leaflets around Paris to announce the birth of the new king of Rome. She flew again that June over the Château de Saint-Cloud to celebrate Napoléon-François-Charles-Joseph Bonaparte's baptism, raining down fireworks from the sky.

> ↤

Sophie's popularity soared, and she began to fly launches in Italy. She transported her balloon across the Alps by coach, and on August 15 of that year performed at the Fête de l'Emperor, a celebration marking Napoléon's forty-second birthday, flying above Milan. The press covered the event widely, inviting the public to glory in what would be Sophie's fortieth flight.

The pressure was on when Napoléon commissioned her to continue to Rome, where Garnerin's Coronation Day balloon had once caused the emperor such embarrassment. Sophie sailed twelve thousand feet above the city, spending the night in her tiny gondola. She reported waking refreshed from a profound sleep before landing quietly at dawn at Tagliacozzo about fifty-five miles away.

Her next flight was over the city of Naples, where she made a difficult ascent in poor weather during a military ceremony overseen by Napoléon's brother-in-law, the king of Naples.

## Napoléon and Balloons

After appointing French artist-inventor Nicolas-Jacques Conté to head the world's first balloon school and factory in 1794—to build balloons for use in the war against Austria—Napoléon seemed to lose interest in manufacturing balloons for military use.

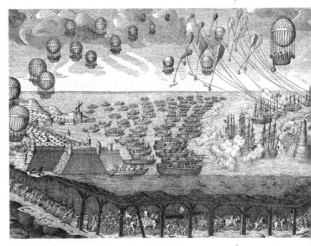

As soon as he returned to France from a campaign in Egypt, in 1799, he abruptly disbanded the French Aerostatic Corps, or Company of Aeronauts— which had run reconnaissance missions during the

*An imagined scene from Napoléon's rumored invasion of England featuring a battalion of balloons*

Battle of Fleurus and other campaigns—and closed the balloon school. Balloons were useful as propaganda went, but erratic and not to be trusted.

Though the emperor had disbanded the French Aerostatic Corps in 1799—and was gearing up for what would ultimately be a failed invasion of Russia, beginning in the spring of 1812—rumors circulated that Napoléon had named Sophie, in addition to her duties as chief aeronaut, "Chief Air Minister of Ballooning." Her mission was to advise on an aerial invasion of England. Sophie predicted that such an attack would fail: France's prevailing westerly winds would hold the balloons back from their target.

Sophie flew at the Third Aeronautical Exhibition held at Champ de Mars, but with many nations riveted by Napoléon's army—advancing toward Moscow at the time—her launch was poorly attended.

She again crossed the Alps with her balloon to make ascents in Italy. One delayed takeoff from Milan in August 1811 pitted her against an impatient official and crowds. As she snipped the cords and shot up into the night air, a gale caught her balloon and whisked it over the Apennine Mountains and toward the coast of Genoa in under an hour.

Dressed in light summer clothing, she trembled with cold as she entered the night clouds at high altitudes. Eventually she spotted an open expanse and worried she had reached the Ligurian Sea. To regain control and avoid being swept off to sure death by drowning, Sophie made preparations to land. There was no ideal spot that close to the forested mountains, but she managed to descend and anchor the balloon to the branch of a tree to keep from blowing back up into the clouds.

As she drifted off to sleep in her balloon car, Sophie had no idea that she had landed near the tiny mountain village of Montebruno, which had experienced another remarkable visitation in 1478 when an apparition of the Virgin Mary had appeared and a shrine was built in her honor.

By morning, local farmers and shepherds had noted the strange object in the trees, and word spread quickly through the village.

Sophie must have been bewildered, waking up in a circle of reverent locals. One observer wrote to the prefect of Genoa:

> *Last night at nine hours after noon, the balloon departed from Milan landed here. On board there was M.me Blanchard, it descended in a wild wood called "la Fricea," one and a half mile from Montebruno. This morning, at the break of dawn, some of the locals saw this machine, while they took their cattle to the pasture, and took it for a miracle sent from heaven, some for the Virgin Mary, some for thieves, but in their uncertainties they decided to inform the Mayor. When the son of the Mayor arrived on the spot he saw a man was holding this woman in his arms and was venerating her as the Virgin Mary: he told him to let her go.*

Sophie spent the day in Montebruno and left on the seventeenth for Torriglia, where a curious priest pointed her toward Genoa. Many spoke French there, and Sophie found a hospitable welcome.

➤  ◄

The independent and intrepid Sophie always flew alone, though "selling a seat" in her balloon would have brought in additional income. She had sound sponsorship and preferred to master her own destiny.

But no early balloonist was ever truly the master of her or his fate.

Early aeronauts had no detailed maps of flight paths, none of the precise data about atmospheric pressure, wind direction, and turbulence that modern pilots rely on, and, of course, that old devil navigation still eluded them. Balloons went where the wind wanted them to go, and the dangers of life on the wing were real and ever-present.

Sophie sometimes passed out during high-altitude flights or suffered nosebleeds, determined to travel upward of twelve thousand feet when she could, even if it meant being deprived of oxygen.

She came close to freezing to death on numerous occasions, waking with her hands and face covered in frost or icicles.

The whims of weather sometimes forced her to climb higher and higher still, at times passing out in the process—or staying airborne for up to fourteen and a half hours to avoid being trapped in a hailstorm. One flight nearly drowned her when she crashed in a marsh and found herself tangled in balloon netting.

But word of these near-fatal exploits only added to her allure. Sophie seemed invincible, and this magic kept her in the limelight. More than anything she hated to disappoint her fans, and she might have inherited some of her husband's well-known wariness for sharing the stage with rivals.

Back in Paris in the summer of 1812, Sophie received a letter from André-Jacques Garnerin, inviting her to dinner at the Hôtel de Colennes to chat about "a project that might be of mutual interest." He might have hoped to merge their entertainment empires (and recover his good name) by staging ascents and parachute drops above the Jardin du Tivoli or Parc Monceau featuring Sophie and his niece, Élisa, but there is no record of Sophie's reply.

➤ ◄

Throughout Europe and the United Kingdom, the perils of ballooning continued to make headlines.

On October 9, 1812, British balloonist James Sadler, who had piloted many successful flights in England, crashed into the sea and was fished out near Holyhead (his son would also die in a balloon accident a few years later). Pioneering Italian balloonist Francesco Zambeccari died during an 1812 ascent when his balloon snagged in trees and caught fire, with the balloonist taking a fatal leap to try to escape.

But most general headlines of the day tracked Napoléon's doomed assault on Russia. Tsar Alexander I refused to surrender, leaving Napoléon's army to endure a long Russian winter and dwindling supplies.

In November 1812, Napoléon abandoned his troops and returned to Paris, opening the way for further defeats and leading to his abdication of the throne on April 11, 1814. When Napoléon was banished to the Mediterranean island of Elba, the French monarchy seized the opportunity to reclaim the throne, restoring the Bourbon king, Louis XVIII, as leader of France.

*Sophie Blanchard flies for the restored Bourbon king, Louis XVIII, 1814.*

For Sophie, the show went on. She wowed the new king with her spectacular May 4, 1814, flight from Paris's Pont Neuf, taking off in a haze of fireworks and Bengal lights—a slow-burning pyrotechnics display—and releasing a flurry of white pigeons that, "like the dove of the ark," wrote one reporter, "flew to communicate to the provinces that the storms and tempests of France were at an end."

Louis XVIII at once followed Napoléon's lead and dubbed Sophie "Official Aeronaut of the Restoration."

Though there was some temporary shuffling of leadership that year (Napoléon escaped and stole back the French throne for one hundred days, but lost once and for all at the Battle of Waterloo in June 1815), Sophie must have been only too happy to accept the new king's offer. Her loyalty was to ballooning, and with warlike Napoléon finally silenced, the people of Paris wanted festivals and distractions.

For Sophie, there would be years of marvelous public displays to come. The evening *fêtes* at pleasure gardens like Tivoli—a favorite entertainment for adults in Parisian high society—were a place to see and be seen, to take a thrilling ride on early-model roller coasters and Ferris wheels, and enjoy music, dancing, magicians, and marionettes. One traveler at the time described a night of theater and ropedancers, and a fireworks finale like "a radiant sun," with "blazing fires all around" and "a long, slow, and heavy fall of golden sparks."

*A crowd views fireworks at a Bastille Day* fête *in Paris like those Sophie regularly performed at. A balloon appears in the upper right corner.*

124

But when Sophie headlined at Tivoli, her balloon prowess and stunning pyrotechnics—rockets, cascades, complex strings of Bengal lights ignited with fuses—stole the show. The tiny and by all appearances fragile aeronaut seemed to hover, like a dove, hundreds of feet above the crowd in a swirl of smoke and colored light.

MORT DE M<sup>ME</sup> BLANCHARD (1819)

*Collector's card illustration*
*of Sophie's fateful last flight*

# CHAPTER 15

# Sinister Presentiments

*July 6, 1819*

In French author Jules Verne's fictional story "A Drama in the Air," the narrator finds himself up in a balloon piloted by a madman. " 'Did you see Madame Blanchard fall?' " the pilot demands, his hair "disheveled" and his eyes haggard. " 'I saw her; yes, I! I was at Tivoli on the sixth of July, 1819.' "

The narrator listens in mounting horror. The "disheveled" mad-man has an uncanny knowledge of early balloon disasters. " 'My eyes were fixed upon her,' " he recalls, wild-eyed. " 'Suddenly an unexpected gleam lit up the darkness. I thought she was preparing a surprise.' "

➤ ↞

Many eyewitnesses thought the same that summer night in Paris.

It was a hot, overcast evening. As Sophie readied for one of her acclaimed ascents at the Jardin du Tivoli, she packed into her balloon gondola an unusual amount of "Bengal fire," a slow-burning pyrotechnics display.

With the orchestra loud in the bandstand below, friends and bystanders mouthed misgivings—did she really need to pack so much firepower?

Sophie seemed gravely determined to go up. She needed the Bengal fire to spotlight her balloon against cloudy skies.

She also seemed uncharacteristically nervous. Sophie was forty-one, "still young, sprightly, and amiable," according to one acquaintance. She was confident and skilled, a superstar of the skies, but yes, she had misgivings of her own that night.

One magazine reported later that before takeoff, "Madame Blanchard, commonly so courageous, was agitated by sinister presentiments. At the moment of her ascent she told someone near her— 'I know not why, but I am not tranquil to-day.'"

After deliberating a long while, she made her choice: *"Allons,"* she said, *"ce sera pour la dernière fois."*

*Let's go, this will be for the last time.*

➤ ◄

Luminous in her trademark white dress and ostrich-plumed hat, carrying a torch and a white flag, Sophie stepped into her gondola as the orchestra music in the pit swelled and fireworks brightened the sky. In an instant, unexpectedly strong winds lifted her away from the gardens.

At about five hundred feet and rising rapidly, Sophie set off her rockets and Bengal lights. Tiny parachute bombs rained shivering silver over Paris. Fire shot up from the top of the balloon with a flash and a pop, and her applauding fans gasped and cried, "Beautiful! Beautiful!" They chanted, as they often did, *"Vive Madame Blanchard!"*

Sophie knew that the hydrogen in the mouth of her balloon had caught fire. In one report, her craft lit "up Paris like some immense moving beacon," though many still thought the spectacle was part of the show. They clapped and cheered as wind blew the flaming balloon along. It was going down at a slant, skimming the tops of buildings.

Jules Verne re-created the scene in his short story "A Drama in the Air":

*The light flashed out, suddenly disappeared and reappeared, and gave the summit of the balloon the shape of an immense jet of ignited gas. This sinister glow shed itself over the Boulevard and the whole Montmartre quarter. Then I saw the unhappy woman rise, try twice to close the appendage of the balloon, so as to put out the fire, then sit down in her car and try to guide her descent; for she did not fall. The combustion of the gas lasted for several minutes. The balloon, becoming gradually less, continued to descend, but it was not a fall. The wind blew from the north-west and drove it towards Paris.*

But at some point the "dreadful blaze struck terror into the hearts of all the spectators," reported the English *Gentleman's Review,* "leaving them in but little doubt as to the deplorable fate of the unfortunate aeronaut." The strong canopy held long enough for Sophie to cut ballast and slow her descent, and for a moment, it seemed the invincible aeronaut might land a miracle.

Then the balloon basket caught on the slanting roof of number 16, rue de Provence. Sophie tipped out, snared in her balloon netting, and slid along the roof. One eyewitness claimed that she caught hold of a parapet and dangled with enough composure to call for help—"*À moi, à moi!*"—before crashing to the cobbles.

An English tourist saw everything from his nearby hotel window:

*For a few minutes, the balloon was concealed by clouds. Presently it reappeared, and there was seen a momentary sheet of flame. . . . In a few seconds, the poor creature, enveloped and entangled in the netting of her machine, fell with a frightful crash upon the slanting roof of a house in the Rue de Provence . . . and thence into the street, and Madame Blanchard was taken up a shattered corpse!*

The fire in the balloon went out on impact, and Sophie's body was not burned. Her hat and a shoe were found on the roof.

>➤ ⤛

Accounts of her blazing fall from the skies over Paris ran in newspapers across Europe as well as in England and America. "It is impossible to describe the scene which Tivoli now presented," wrote one. "Cries of lamentation burst from all sides; numbers of females fell into convulsions—consternation was depicted in every face."

It was a theatrical end to a theatrical life.

Tivoli shut down for the night, calling a halt to festivities and organizing a collection for the beloved balloonist's family. The public subscription raised two thousand francs, but Sophie had no family. Her will earmarked fifty francs for the eight-year-old daughter of a family friend. The donation funded a monument over Sophie's tombstone in the Ninety-Fourth Division of Père Lachaise Cemetery in Paris. A sphere topped with fire and symbolizing her flaming balloon rises from the pedestal.

The monument's inscription, VICTIME DE SON ART ET DE SON INTRÉPIDITÉ, translates to "Victim of her art and her intrepidity."

Sophie had sacrificed all for a brief, bold life in the air.

*Panoramic view of a balloon over Paris*

# AFTERWORD

The shocking death of "Royal Aeronaut" and aerial pioneer Sophie Blanchard hurt the reputation of ballooning in France and around the world. Her career had already outlasted the 1780s height of "balloono-mania" that riveted Europe and England and inspired a great many artists, authors, and dreamers.

Sophie wasn't the first woman in the air, but she was the first to make an independent living there. After her husband's death, she flew alone. She piloted sixty-seven spectacular flights under always-dangerous conditions.

Her last was as heartbreaking as it was breathtaking and gave some critics the chance to scoff. "A tale of disaster like that of Madame Blanchard," wrote American poet and lawyer Grenville Mellon in 1828, "is dire proof that a woman in a balloon is either out of her element, or too high in it."

Early male aeronauts, too, routinely risked their lives to slip free from the tyranny of gravity. A great many, like Sophie, became victims of their "art and intrepidity." Were women held accountable for more because less was expected of them? Did Mellon fault Sophie for falling? Or for daring to fly in the first place?

Sophie's sensational end was traumatic for her fans and followers. But she did the work in full awareness of the risks and sacrifices.

Was the birdlike girl who liked to soar alone at night a "victim" of her art? Or was she a dreamer, an adventurer with a practical eye to her own happiness, however fleeting? Like her husband and mentor, Jean-Pierre Blanchard—who chose as his professional motto the Latin phrase *Sic itur ad astra*—"Thus you shall go to the stars"—she made her choice and dedicated her life to it.

We all get to choose.

Do we remember Sophie for falling? Or for flying?

# ACKNOWLEDGMENTS

Thanks to my wise agent Jill Grinberg and to the whole high-flying team at Jill Grinberg Literary Management; to dear friend and fellow research geek Lisa Goodfellow, who knows where to find answers (to even the most arcane questions); to Random House Studio for supporting this eccentric story, and to my fearless editor, Ann Kelley, who always nudges me to the next level; to designers Andrea Lau and Larsson McSwain for the gorgeous interiors and book jacket respectively; to copy editors Alison Kolani (indexer extraordinaire!) and Barbara Perris and proofreaders Nancee Adams and Jackie Hornberger for their keen bird's-eye view at many stages of production; to Tisha Paul, Tim Terhune, and Charlotte Roos for countless things; and to the folks in Sales and Marketing who'll see the sum of our labors out into the world. Thanks, finally, to the archives and the many writers and researchers who helped me reconstruct the history of balloonomania and give voice to a little-known aviation pioneer. Of special note are the bountiful Tissandier Collection at the Library of Congress, and author-historian Richard Holmes, whose lively *The Age of Wonder* and *Falling Upwards* were indispensable.

# TIMELINE

**1765-1783**

American Revolution

**December 1776**

American diplomat Benjamin Franklin arrives in France.

**March 25, 1778**

Marie Madeleine-Sophie Armant, later known as Sophie Blanchard, is born in southern coastal France.

**June 1783**

First recorded hot-air balloon flight; Annonay, France

**August 1783**

First recorded hydrogen balloon flight; Paris, France

**September 19, 1783**

First recorded hot-air flight with animal passengers; Versailles, France

**November 21, 1783**

First piloted hot-air flight; Jean-François Pilâtre de Rozier and Marquis d'Arlandes; Paris, France

## December 1, 1783
First piloted hydrogen flight; Jacques Alexandre César Charles and Marie-Noël Robert; Paris, France

## March 2, 1784
Debut flight of Jean-Pierre Blanchard; Paris, France

## June 4, 1784
Élisabeth Thible is the first woman to take flight; Lyon, France.

## June 24, 1784
Edward Warren, a thirteen-year-old boy, is the first American to ascend—in a balloon built by attorney Peter Carnes; Baltimore.

## January 7, 1785
Jean-Pierre Blanchard and Dr. John Jeffries fly over the English Channel; Dover, England.

## June 15, 1785
Jean-François Pilâtre de Rozier and Pierre Romain are the first aeronauts to die in a balloon accident.

## 1789-1799
French Revolution

## January 9, 1793
Jean-Pierre Blanchard's celebrated balloon voyage in America; Philadelphia

## June 26, 1794
During the Battle of Fleurus, the French Army sends up a tethered hydrogen balloon, *l'Entreprenant,* to track the movements of the Austrian Army.

## October 22, 1797

André-Jacques Garnerin takes the first recorded parachute jump from a balloon; Paris, France.

## 1804–1809

Sophie Armant marries Jean-Pierre Blanchard and becomes an aeronaut.

## June 1805

Sophie Blanchard takes her first solo flight; France.

## March 1809

Jean-Pierre Blanchard dies after being injured in a balloon accident.

## 1810–1814

Sophie Blanchard is Emperor Napoléon Bonaparte's "Aeronaut of the Official Festivals."

## 1814–1819

Sophie Blanchard is King Louis XVIII's "Official Aeronaut of the Restoration."

## July 6, 1819

Sophie Blanchard dies in a balloon accident; Paris, France.

# BIBLIOGRAPHY

"Abstract of Foreign Occurrences," *The Gentleman's Magazine,* Volume 126, 1819.

Adams, John Quincy. *Diary of John Quincy Adams,* Volume 1, November 1779, March 1786. masshist.org/publications/adams-papers/index.php/view/DQA01d585

Anderson, James M. *Daily Life During the French Revolution.* Westport, CT: Greenwood Press, 2007.

"The annual register, or a view of the history, politics, and literature, for the years 1784 and 1785." *Historical Texts.* London: J. Dodsley, 1795.

Blanchard, Jean-Pierre. "Journal of my forty-fifth ascension, being the first performed in America, on the ninth of January, 1793." archive.org/search.php?query=creator%3A%22Blanchard%2C+Jean-Pierre%2C+1753-1809%22

Cavallo, Tiberius. "Description of a Meteor, Observed Aug. 18, 1783. By Mr. Tiberius Cavallo, F. R. S." *Philosophical Transactions of the Royal Society of London.* Vol. 74 (1784), 108–111.

*Chambers's Journal.* United Kingdom, W. & R. Chambers, 1851.

Covington, Richard. "Marie Antoinette," *Smithsonian Magazine,* November 2006. smithsonianmag.com/history/marie-antoinette-134629573

Crouch, Tom D. "The Ascent of the Great Montgolfier Balloon." Smithsonian National Air and Space Museum.

Darling, David. *Mayday!: A History of Flight Through Its Martyrs, Oddballs and Daredevils.* New York: Simon and Schuster, 2015.

Ford, Lily. "For the Sake of the Prospect." *Public Domain Review.* publicdomainreview.org/essay/for-the-sake-of-the-prospect-experiencing-the-world-from-above-in-the-late-18th-century

founders.archives.gov/documents/Washington/05-11-02-0383

geriwalton.com/sophie-blanchard-first-female-fly-balloon-solo

Glines, C. V. "First in America's Skies." historynet.com/jean-pierre-blanchard
-made-first-us-aerial-voyage-in-1793.htm

Holmes, Richard. *The Age of Wonder: How the Romantic Generation Discovered
the Beauty and Terror of Science.* New York: Pantheon Books, 2008.

Holmes, Richard. *Falling Upwards: How We Took to the Air.* New York: Pantheon
Books, 2013.

Jackson, Donald Dale. *The Aeronauts: The Epic of Flight.* Alexandria, VA: Time-
Life Books, 1981.

Kotar, S. L., and J. E. Gessler. *Ballooning: A History 1782–1900.* Jefferson, NC, and
London: McFarland & Company, 2011.

Lausanne, Edita. *The Romance of Ballooning: The Story of the Early Aeronauts.*
New York: Viking Press, 1971.

Lynn, Michael R. *The Sublime Invention: Ballooning in Europe, 1783–1820.*
London: Pickering and Chatto, 2010.

"Madam Blanchard, the Aeronaut." *Scientific American,* Supplement Number 195,
Volume 8, September 27, 1879.

Marion, F. *Wonderful Balloon Ascents.* New York: Cassell Petter & Galpin, 1870.
archive.org/details/wonderfulballona00mariuoft/page/n8/mode/2up

Mellon, Grenville. *Sad Tales and Glad Tales.* Boston: S. G. Goodrich, 1828.

mountvernon.org/library/digitalhistory/digital-encyclopedia/article/george
-washington-and-ballooning

Ovid. "Daedalus and Icarus." *Metamorphosis,* Book VIII: 183–235. ovid.lib
.virginia.edu/trans/Metamorph8.htm#482327661

Pelos, Enrico. *Altavaltrebbia.* "The Strange Story of Sophie Blanchard and
Montebruno." altavaltrebbia.wordpress.com/2011/12/10/the-strange-story-sophie
-blanchard-e-montebruno

Schama, Simon. *Citizens: A Chronicle of the French Revolution.* New York: Random
House, 1990.

*Scientific American* Supplement, Volume 8, No. 195, July 6, 1819.

si.edu/object/ascent-great-montgolfier-balloon%3Anasm_A19680126000

smithsonianmag.com/history/sophie-blanchard-the-high-flying-frenchwoman-who
-revealed-the-thrill-and-danger-of-ballooning-89106237

Tocqueville, Alexis de. *Jacobin.* "A Guide to the French Revolution." jacobinmag
.com/2015/07/french-revolution-bastille-day-guide-jacobins-terror-bonaparte

Verne, Jules. "A Drama in the Air." en.wikisource.org/wiki/Works_of_Jules
_Verne/A_Drama_in_the_Air

Walpole, Horace. "Trial Balloon." *Lapham's Quarterly.* laphamsquarterly.org/discovery/trial-balloon

Walsh, William Shepard. *A Handy Book of Curious Information.* Philadelphia: J. B. Lippincott Company, 1913.

Wright, Sharon. *Balloonomania Belles: Daredevil Divas Who First Took to the Sky.* South Yorkshire, England: Pen & Sword Books Ltd., 2018.

Young, Arthur. *Arthur Young's Travels in France.* London: George Bell and Sons, 1909.

# NOTES

## Introduction

x      "We think of nothing here at present but of flying": Jackson, *The Aeronauts,* 27.

x      "tyranny of gravity": Holmes, *Falling Upwards,* 173.

## 1. A Mysterious Stranger

2      "Listen and mark my words . . . marry her": *Chambers's Journal,* 413.

## 2. The Race Is On

7      "enclose a cloud in a bag": Jackson, 10.

8      "The balloons engross all attention": Jackson, 27.

9      "Within a very few days . . . repeating the fate of Icarus": Holmes, *The Age of Wonder,* 129.

10     "Minos rules all, Icarus . . . I show you!": Ovid, *Metamorphosis,* ovid.lib.virginia.edu/trans/Metamorph8.htm#482327661.

12     "Among our circle of friends . . . journeys in the sky": Jackson, 12.

12     "It rose at once, for some time perpendicular . . . with a great swiftness": Adams, masshist.org/publications/adams-papers/index.php/view/ADMS-03-01-02-0005-0009-0016.

12     "a little Rain had wet it, so that it shone . . . newborn baby?": Jackson, 14.

13     "and if it succeeds it may become very useful to mankind": Adams, masshist.org/publications/adams-papers/index.php/view/ADMS-03-01-02-0005-0009-0016.

13     "The creature, shaking and bounding . . . a long sigh": Lausanne, *The Romance of Ballooning,* 17.

## 3. Much Astonished

18      **"All our views are directed to the air . . . new engines of destruction"**: Walpole, laphamsquarterly.org/discovery/trial-balloon.

19      **"The wicked will of man . . . fellow creatures"**: Walpole, laphamsquarterly.org/discovery/trial-balloon.

19      **"Five thousand . . . speed and impunity"**: Holmes, *The Age of Wonder,* 135–136.

19      **"At last . . . and the air"**: Schama, *Citizens,* 124.

21–22    **"I put on my rouge . . . whole world"** through **"metal-working"**: Covington, smithsonianmag.com/history/marie-antoinette-134629573.

24      **"It was judged . . . much astonished"**: Schama, 123.

## 4. Wide-Open Sky

28      **"like the aurora borealis"** through **"Every object appeared very distinct"**: Cavallo, 109.

29      **"amazing and portentous . . . of this kingdom"**: Schama, 126.

## 5. Perfect Bliss

33      **"The King might be sovereign master . . . men of distinction"**: Schama, 126.

34      **"assured his friends . . . no shock whatsoever"**: Jackson, 19.

35      **"I was surprised . . . the spectators"**: Jackson, 20.

36      **"It is impossible to describe . . . gives way to wonder."**: si.edu/object/ascent-great-montgolfier-balloon%3Anasm_A19680126000.

36      **"On the ground . . . it became democratic"**: Schama, 125.

36–37    **"We must go down!"** through **"*Are you taking this all in?*"**: Holmes, *The Age of Wonder,* 130.

37      **"of considerable size"**: Jackson, 20.

37      **"We had enough fuel . . . hour"**: Holmes, *The Age of Wonder,* 131.

37      **"no shock whatsoever"** through **"the intrepid Pilâtre . . . head"**: Holmes, *The Age of Wonder,* 130.

38      **"a tax on the curiosity of the public"**: Public Domain Review, publicdomainreview.org/essay/for-the-sake-of-the-prospect-experiencing-the-world-from-above-in-the-late-18th-century.

39–40    **"It is for you, *monsieur*"** through **"beneath us presented"**: Jackson, 24.

40      **"I passed in 10 minutes"** through **"in shade"**: Jackson, 25.

41      **"was not a mere delight . . . physical rapture"**: Holmes, *Falling Upwards,* 17.

## 6. The Naked Aeronaut

44    "invention of the Devil." Darling, *Mayday*, 2.

45    "Are you men or gods?": si.edu/object/ascent-great-montgolfier
-balloon%3Anasm_A19680126000.

45    "Covered in sweat . . . and embrace them,": Schama, 130.

## 7. Castles and Arias in the Air

50    "on a building at the fair of St. Laurent . . . lions, tigers, &c.": Wright, 8.

50–51    "flying globes are still . . . prohibited them": Adams, masshist.org/
publications/adams-papers/index.php/view/DQA01d585.

53    "A French peasant . . . harshness of the seasons": Anderson, *The French
Revolution*, 73.

54    "A thousand persons of her sex . . . furnished better proof": Wright, 15.

## 8. A Perilous Crossing

59    "about one hundred and fifty thousand . . . descriptions of people":
Lausanne, 43.

59    "Let posterity know . . . revisited the earth": Holmes, *The Age of
Wonder*, 139.

60    "I am the idol of the whole nation": Holmes, *The Age of Wonder*, 140.

62    "your philosophy seems too bashful": Jackson, 27.

62–63    "for the improvement . . . aerial adventurers": Public Domain
Review, publicdomainreview.org/essay/for-the-sake-of-the-prospect
-experiencing-the-world-from-above-in-the-late-18th-century#ref3.

63    "Dr. Charles' experiment seems decisive" through "no good whatever":
Jackson, 27.

63    "laugh this new . . . possible": Holmes, *The Age of Wonder*, 136.

63–64    "My noble little captain . . . splatter in the water" through "Almost as
naked . . . help us": Lausanne, 48.

64    "hundreds of the first ladies and gentlemen of Paris": Jackson, 33.

## 9. However Dangerous or Difficult

68    "certain of meeting with death": Holmes, *The Age of Wonder*, 154.

68    "a violet flame": Schama, 127.

68    "When they were at an amazing height . . . shocking to mention": "The
annual register," 328.

69    "The Balloonomania . . . Rozier's catastrophe": Wright, 35.

70    "It is said that perhaps he loved glory too much": Schama, 127.

70–71    "The Air Balloon Fun" through "you're depriv'd of your ride: Wright, 19.

71    "The Lady was much frightened" through "with a lady": Wright, 21.

72    "the discouragement so . . . poor Pilâtre de Rozier": Wright, 40.

72    "There is no enterprise . . . constitutes the heroine": Wright, 49.

73    "I feel myself more happy . . . event of my life": Wright, 47–48.

## 10. Revolution!

75    "The poor seem poor indeed . . . no clothes at all": Young, *Arthur Young's Travels Through France,* 125.

76    "The populace is so enraged they would kill for a bushel": Walter, "A Guide to the French Revolution," jacobinmag.com/2015/07/french -revolution-bastille-day-guide-jacobins-terror-bonaparte.

78    "When I came to gather . . . ever observed in the world": Tocqueville, Alexis de. *Jacobin,* jacobinmag.com/2015/07/french-revolution-bastille -day-guide-jacobins-terror-bonaparte.

## 11. Star-Spangled Voyager

88    "the desire of beholding you . . . vast expanse of heaven": Blanchard, "Journal of my forty-fifth ascension," 268.

88    "travelers may hereafter literally pass from country to country on the wings of the wind": Jay, mountvernon.org/library/digitalhistory/digital -encyclopedia/article/george-washington-and-ballooning.

89    "Permit me, gentlemen . . . covered with woods": Glines, "First in America's Skies." historynet.com/jean-pierre-blanchard-made-first-us -aerial-voyage-in-1793.htm.

90    "serene . . ." through "overcast and hazy": Blanchard, 270.

90–91  "leap'd into his boat" through "silence was broke": founders.archives. gov/documents/Washington/05-11-02-0383.

91    "ornamented on one side . . . trembling for his safety": Glines, "First in America's Skies," historynet.com/jean-pierre-blanchard-made-first-us -aerial-voyage-in-1793.htm.

91    "the roofs . . . the roads": Blanchard, 273.

91    "Several Gentlemen gallop'd . . . 20 miles an hour": founders.archives. gov/documents/Washington/05-11-02-0383.

91    "For a long time . . . cries of joy": Blanchard, 273.

91    "divers liquors": Blanchard, 276.

92    "a morsel of biscuit and a glass of wine": Blanchard, 278.

92    "exhilarating juice of the grape" through "hands toward heaven": Blanchard, 280.

92–93  "I have only news paper accts." through "useful to mankind in general": mountvernon.org/library/digitalhistory/digital-encyclopedia/article/ george-washington-and-ballooning.

94       "in the midst . . . to this people!": Blanchard, 280.

94       "we the subscribers saw the bearer . . . Anno Domini, 1793": historynet
.com/jean-pierre-blanchard-made-first-us-aerial-voyage-in-1793.htm.

94       "For some time . . . *same* degree of pleasure from it": historynet.com
/jean-pierre-blanchard-made-first-us-aerial-voyage-in-1793.htm.

94–95   "I therefore make an end . . . caps, aprons, and umbrellas": Jackson, 48.

## 12. A New Emperor and the First Family of the Clouds

100      "was no more scandal" through "the next ten days": Walsh, 11.

101–102  "This evening Mr. and Mrs. Garnerin" through "her new voyage":
Wright, 139.

102      "Every eye was turned" through "a similar danger": Wright, 140.

103      "a programme of games and races resembling those of antiquity": Ernest
John Knapton, *Empress Josephine,* New York: Harvard University Press,
1963, p. 248.

## 13. Incomparable Sensation!

108      "birdlike": Holmes, *Falling Upwards,* 46.

108      *"Sensation incomparable!"*: Holmes, *Falling Upwards,* 41.

109      "majestically and without danger": Kotar/Gessler, 81.

110      "seriously angry" through "her assistance": Kotar/Gessler, 82.

111–112  "movement at first was slow" through "with much kindness assisted her":
geriwalton.com/sophie-blanchard-first-female-fly-balloon-solo.

112      "no fatal consequences were apprehended . . . on one ear": Wright, 55.

112      "stood by him during . . . help himself": *Scientific American* Supplement,
Volume 8, No. 195, July 6, 1819, 3099.

112      "My poor dear . . . into the water": Jackson, 48.

113      "valiantly . . . she had lost": *Scientific American* Supplement, 3099.

## 14. Storms and Tempests

115–116  "heavy machine" through "amusement to him and his wife": *Chambers's
Journal,* 413.

121      "Last night . . . let her go": Pelos, altavaltrebbia.wordpress.
com/2011/12/10/the-strange-story-sophie-blanchard-e-montebruno.

122      "a project that might be of mutual interest": Holmes, *Falling Upwards,* 43.

124      "like the dove of the ark . . . were at an end": Kotar/Gessler, *Ballooning:
A History 1782–1900,* 84.

124      "a radiant sun" through "heavy fall of golden sparks": Madame Domeier,
*An Appendix to the Descriptions of Paris,* London: Samuel Leigh, 1820,
p. 61.

## 15. Sinister Presentiments

## Afterword

# PICTURE CREDITS

72      Wikimedia Commons

74      Wikimedia Commons

77      Library of Congress Prints and Photographs Division, LC-USZC4-5913

80      Library of Congress Prints and Photographs Division, LC-USZ62-1409

81      Wikimedia Commons

83      Library of Congress Prints and Photographs Division, LC-USZ62-65649

86      Library of Congress Prints and Photographs Division, LC-USZ62–110394

89      Rijksmuseum

96      Wikimedia Commons

99      Library of Congress Prints and Photographs Division, LC-DIG-
        ppmsca-02504

101     Library of Congress Prints and Photographs Division, LC-DIG-
        ppmsca-02548

103     Wikimedia Commons

106     Library of Congress Prints and Photographs Division, LC-DIG-
        ppmsca-02179

109     Library of Congress Prints and Photographs Division, LC-DIG-
        ppmsca-02233

110     Wikimedia Commons

113     Rijksmuseum

114     Library of Congress Prints and Photographs Division, LC-DIG-
        ppmsca-02180

119     Pictorial Press Ltd / Alamy Stock Photo

123     Library of Congress Prints and Photographs Division, LC-DIG-ds-04683

124     Library of Congress Prints and Photographs Division, LC-DIG-
        ppmsca-02626

126     Library of Congress Prints and Photographs Division

132     Wellcome Collection

# INDEX

Page numbers in *italics* refer to illustrations.

Blanchard, Jean-Pierre *(cont'd.)*
  debut flight of, 43–44
  financial troubles of, 94–95, 108,
    113
  first English flight with a woman
    aboard, 71
  flights in America of, *86,* 87–94
  glory seeking by, 44
  injuries and illnesses of, 111, 112
  as inventor, 5
  motto of, 134
  parachutes and, 98
  "passport" from George
    Washington of, 93–94
  self-promotion of, 57
Blanchard, Sophie, x, *106, 113, 114,*
    *123*
  bravery while flying of, 116
  childhood of, xi, 1, *26,* 27, 29–30,
    43, 51, 53–54, 55, 63, 75, 76, 84,
    107–108
  dangers faced by, 122, 133–134
  death of, *126,* 127–130, 133–134
  fears and anxieties of, 27, 29, 108,
    115–116, 117, 128
  final flight of, *126,* 127–130,
    133–134
  first ride in a hot-air balloon of,
    107–108
  first solo flight of, 111–112
  flights in honor of Louis XVIII of,
    *123,* 123–124
  independent ballooning career of,
    113, 116–125, 133
  as Jean-Pierre's ballooning assistant,
    108–109, 111
  popularity of, 118–119
  role as Napoléon's chief aeronaut
    of, 116–117, 120

  role as Official Aeronaut of the
    Restoration of, 124
  tombstone of, 130
Bonaparte, Napoléon, *96,* 97–98,
    102–104, 108, 110, 111,
    116–120, 123–124
  abdication and banishment of, 123
  aggression of, 117
  assault on Russia by, 123
  birthday celebration of, 118–119
  divorce of, 116
  as emperor, 98, 103–104, 116,
    118–120
  son of, 118
Bonaparte, Napoléon-François-
    Charles-Joseph, 118
Bordeaux, France, 110
Boulogne, France, 67, *69*
Britain, *see* England
Brittany, France, ix–x

# C

Calais, France, *56,* 64
Callet, Antoine-François, 81
Carnes, Peter, 87–88
Catholic Church, 76–79, 84, 98
Cavallo, Tiberius, 6–7, 28, 62
Central Bureau of Police, 100
*Ceres* (ship), 87
Champ de Mars, 12, 43, 118, 120
Charles, Jacques, 11–12, 13, 17, *35,*
    *38–41, 40,* 43, *45,* 49, 57, 63
  as "father of the gas balloon," 11
  financing of, 38
Château de Saint-Cloud, 118
Cholmondeley, Lord, 70
comets, 28–29, *28*
Conté, Nicolas-Jacques, 119

# ABOUT THE AUTHOR

Deborah Noyes is the author of numerous books for young readers, including *A Hopeful Heart: Louisa May Alcott Before Little Women*, a CCBC Notable Book; *The Magician and the Spirits*, a *Washington Post* Best Children's Book of the Year; and *Ten Days a Madwoman*, called "irresistible" in a starred review from *School Library Journal*. A friend once brought Deborah up in a hot-air balloon for her birthday, and she never forgot the feeling. Someday she'd like to spend a whole night alone in the clouds, as Sophie often did. *Sensation incomparable*!